Dugout Wisdom:
The Ten Principles
of Championship Teams

Jim Murphy

ISBN: 1-58518-768-2
Library of Congress Control Number: 2002115792

Book layout: Jennifer Bokelmann
Cover design: Kerry Hartjen
Front cover photo: Otto Gruele Jr./Getty Images
Illustrations (pages 23-24): © Gary Adams

Coaches Choice
P.O. Box 1828
Monterey, CA 93942
www.coacheschoice.com

Dedication

This book is dedicated to the memory of my great friend and teammate Brandy Pugh, who got me into coaching.

Acknowledgments

First, I'd like to thank God for all He has done in my life. I'd also like to thank my parents for their lifelong love and support, and the following people for their help with the book: my mother Michiko, brother Patrick, Dale Bracewell, Kevin Lawrence, my advisor Dr. Richard Mosher, Jennifer Webb, my Mastermind group, and all the coaches who took the time to sit down with me and share their philosophies.

This book is about seeking excellence. Phillippians 4:8 says it well: "Finally, brethren, whatever is true, whatever is honorable, whatever is right, whatever is pure, whatever is lovely, whatever is of good repute, if there is any excellence and if anything worthy of praise, dwell on these things."

Preface

This book started as the dream of a graduate student. It was the spring of 1998 and with the support of my personal coach Kevin Lawrence, I decided that for my master's degree in coaching science I was going to meet and learn from the best managers and coaches in the game.

I think to become the best, you've got to find out who the best is, meet him (or her), study him, learn how he thinks, how he acts, and emulate him. I flew to San Diego, Phoenix, and Florida—all funded by my student loan and a handy credit card—to chase down these managers and coaches.

Getting my contact information off the Internet, I got in touch with many of the top managers in the game. While in Florida, I put about 500 miles a day on the rental car, I braved a tornado that had killed 36 people a few weeks earlier, and I got to hang with Davey Johnson at his house, where we did his interview.

Some teams did everything they could to help me out, especially the San Francisco Giants, Florida Marlins, Baltimore Orioles, and Los Angeles Dodgers. It was an amazing process for me, a big baseball fan. With most teams, I had full access to the clubhouse, the press box, any seat in the stadium during the game, and occasionally field access.

To interview Gene Mauch, I met him during pre-game batting practice behind the batting cage. Cecil Fielder and Tim Salmon were hitting bombs out of the yard, Rod Carew was behind me working with a hitter off the tee, and Larry Bowa was next to me talking to another coach. That was pretty cool.

I had to chase some managers down. To talk to Felipe Alou, I had to sneak in the back door. (We ended up just chatting—he wanted to meet up during the season but our schedules didn't match.) I ran after Larry Dierker, I interviewed Phil Garner with the Hall of Fame people waiting for us to finish, and I sat in the dugout with Jim Leyland telling jokes before the interview. Tom Kelly called me at home, and Dusty Baker signed his book and gave it to me. I interviewed Sparky Anderson while we were surrounded by autograph seekers, with the microphone in his face as he signed and talked. I interviewed Mike Hargrove behind the batting cage, and Art Howe in the weight room. Skip Bertman invited me into the locker room for his pre-game speech and video before a regional playoff game.

Others I didn't have time to interview. The Dodgers wanted me to stay for a few days to get a real feel for their system. (I couldn't because I had to fly out the next day.) By coincidence, Cam Bonifay of the Pittsburgh Pirates was out of town when I arrived and returned when I left. It was all quite an experience for a lifelong baseball fan.

I learned a lot doing the groundwork for this book. I learned to be bold, and if you have a dream and you're sincere, organized, and persistent, people will go out of their way to help you. If you courageously pursue your dreams, the universe must comply.

— JM

Contents

Dedication...3

Acknowledgments...4

Preface 5

Foreword 8

Chapter 1: Build Individual Champions 9

Chapter 2: Form a Covenant...20

Chapter 3: Vividly Imagine the End Result...35

Chapter 4: Develop Team Chemistry..50

Chapter 5: Coach the Details..68

Chapter 6: Win the Pitch: Setting Goals 82

Chapter 7: Practice Under Pressure..94

Chapter 8: Excel in the Exclusive Moment..104

Chapter 9: Seek Greatness Through Adversity...123

Chapter 10: Motivate Daily...142

Appendix: Individuals Who Were Interviewed for This Book............................161

Endnotes 167

About the Author...169

Foreword

I first met Jim four years ago through Pat Gillick. Jim was doing his master's degree in human kinetics and for it he wanted to study the game he loved from the best in the business.

Jim and I sat down in my living room and for two hours I explained to him what I've learned through the years, from my playing days in the World Series to managing the 1986 World Series champion New York Mets, and winning the American League Manager of the Year award in 1997.

We discussed a range of issues, from how to succeed under pressure, to how I handle discipline, to what kind of goals I set. Basically, I told him what my philosophy is, and how I implement that with my teams.

For example, I talked about building a championship team. It's not about signing the best young players—it's about taking players with good raw talent and giving them a good environment in which to develop. It's about helping players develop into 'gamers'—the type of player that doesn't shy away when the pressure is on, who will give you all he has. Those guys provide the chemistry that is so important to becoming a winning team. If you don't get the right chemistry, the right mix, and the right guy coaching, it's a shot in the dark.

Most coaches have a pretty good idea about the X's and O's. The great managers and coaches also have a good grasp of things like handling the players, developing team chemistry, learning to use all 25 guys, and keeping players motivated and always ready.

Dugout Wisdom includes interviews with some of the best managers in baseball, from legendary professional coaches like Sparky Anderson and Gene Mauch, to more recent guys like Jim Leyland, Dusty Baker, Tom Kelly, and Art Howe. The book also features legends of the college game, guys like Rod Dedeaux, Skip Bertman, Jerry Kindall, and Ron Polk.

With *Dugout Wisdom*, Jim has done for coaches, players, and fans what we all would love to do: pick the brains of the top managers in the game and ask them their secrets, their philosophies.

— Davey Johnson

CHAPTER 1

Build Individual Champions

"To build champions, you need to build their entire lives around excellence."
— Skip Bertman
Five-time NCAA Division I national champion,
Louisiana State University

In baseball, more than almost any other sport, two things are apparent: players are going to fail every day, and the game will often come down to the last batter in the lineup, or even the last guy on the bench. It's not a sport where a team can rely on their star player in the last minute of the game: to win a championship in baseball, a team has to have all 25 guys contributing, accepting their roles, and putting the team first.

If the 25 guys have mental toughness and are conscientious, then they'll be able to persevere when times are tough, respect each other, and inspire each other, lifting their game to new unimagined heights. They'll be more determined to not give in, in a game when players so often want to, if they know they can count on their teammates and their teammates can count on them.

A coach that believes in his team can instill this kind of faith between players. If teammates have integrity and continually strive for excellence, then together they can achieve much more than they might have imagined. They can become champions.

A championship team in baseball is really only as strong as its weakest link. There's no telling when a player will be needed; the last guy on the bench will get called upon sooner or later. When he is called upon, if he's not ready it could cost the game, or even the season. The idea is to build champions out of every single player on the roster.

What is a Champion?

Champions have, among other things, the courage to believe in their dreams, the desire to make their dreams a reality, the integrity to do what is right, the cognitive ability to know the details of the game, the resilience to keep getting up, the determination to not give in, and the self-discipline to do what is necessary. This list can be summed up by one word – character. Character includes what a player is made of, how he performs in challenging circumstances, and how he acts when everything goes against him. These elements may be just as important as, or even more important than raw talent. Players may be chock full of physical ability, but character is what separates the wheat from the chaff.

One young quarterback, coming out of the University of Notre Dame, was deemed slow on his feet, with only an average arm. That young quarterback of supposedly average talent led the San Francisco 49ers to four Super Bowl victories. Joe Montana had instinct. Desire. Poise. Cognitive ability. He had character.

Champions Have Character

The mental toughness and perseverance that is so closely linked to character is tapped by the great coaches who capitalize on their players' potential. Andy Lopez, who led Pepperdine to the NCAA Division I title in 1992 (now at the University of Arizona), works on the character of his players constantly. "The longer I coach, the more I come to realize that makeup is probably more important than anything else," Lopez says. "If all things are equal, and you have better makeup than me, you're going to beat me. Every day of my life, my challenge is to get my kids stronger and more courageous.

"My technique is to talk about the mental approach a lot, mental aggressiveness. I talk about Patton, Billy Martin [guys like that]. If I see a great article, I'll post it in the clubhouse, make sure they read about this guy's makeup, and so forth. A couple years ago, there was an article in the New York Times on David Cone. The headline read, 'Cone's teammates say he has the heart of a lion.' I remember cutting it out and posting it in the clubhouse and asking, "Can we say this about you?"

When teammates can say that about each other, it opens the door for a host of opportunities. Players will be willing to go the extra distance for each other, in practice and in games. Teammates with mutual respect support each other, and they unite in a way that creates an energy seen only on the best teams.

Bob Bennett, former head coach at Fresno State University, explains the importance of character: "The critical thing for me after talent is character, because you win with good character. People with good character will do stuff the right way and they will care about each other and the team. If you don't do that, what happens is you might have good players who could be something 'if only.' You don't have to say 'if only' about a guy with character. You say he did the best he could, and the best he could is always good enough if he has decent ability. You've probably seen a superstar that wasn't a very good team player, and another guy who was a .270 hitter, but you say in a clutch situation, 'I'd rather have that guy up than anybody on my team.' You know he's pulling for you and he's pulling for everybody else."

Having a player with character is vital for many reasons. For example, in baseball, where so much time is spent together, a little negativity can easily spread. And with such a long season, there will be down times, times when people don't get along, times when the team faces adversity. If everyone is pulling in different directions, the team can't create momentum. Character brings so many positives to the team. It has a snowball effect, similar to how a positive (or negative) thought generates many other similar thoughts. Good character does not stand alone.

Mike Hargrove, manager for the Baltimore Orioles, puts more emphasis on character than talent: "I would rather have a player with a whole lot of character and a little bit of talent as opposed to a player with a whole lot of talent and very little character. The people with a lot of character and little talent are going to overachieve and get more out of their talent. It's a more enjoyable process in getting that effort out of them. Also, when you're standing against the wall and you're in a mud storm, and you look up and you have all your players, all the people you really count on, standing there taking their share of the shots, when it's all over with, you clean yourself off and you go on and you're better for it. People with no character, they say 'I'll stay with you, I'll stay with you,' and then when the mud starts flying, you look up and they're hiding behind the wall. Once the mud storm's over, they run out and say, 'Let's go get 'em.' I don't have any use for people like that. I think people like that are never going to seize the moment; they're always looking for an excuse, a way out. They're not going to stay focused. And once their talent starts getting away from them, they don't know how to make their talent work."

Baseball involves so much failure that players have to learn to deal with the doubts that a slump brings. If a player doesn't have the inner strength that keeps him persevering, working hard, and pulling for his teammates, then it's easy for him to become negative. He may develop self pity and withdraw from the team, thereby forcing his teammates to carry the load. Players with character will work a little harder to overcome adversity, and inspire their teammates to do the same.

Pat Gillick, general manager for the Seattle Mariners, has won everywhere he's gone. He took the Blue Jays to back-to-back World Series championships, brought the Orioles to the playoffs, then went to Seattle and led the Mariners to the best record in the history of major league baseball.

Gillick explains the importance of character: "I look for players with a combination of character and ability. I think if you're going to build a team, character means a great deal in professional sports. It might even mean more than physical ability. I think you have to set the tone for the organization, and one of the ways [to do that] is with the type of people you have in the organization. In pro sports, work ethic is very important. You need someone that's going to set a tone, someone that shows up to work every day, that handles themselves in a professional manner on the field. This, in some ways, is more important than actual physical talent."

Jerry Kindall, who won three national championships at the University of Arizona, says that two of the three qualities he looks for in recruits are intangible: "academic responsibility and integrity (physical talent is the third). He explains: "I look at their physical skills and academic responsibility. I also want to make a personal home visit. I want to see how they react to their parents. I want to see respect and courtesy, to their siblings and especially their parents. That combination of physical skill, academic responsibility, and awareness of respect to others. That's a guy we like to get."

Developing the Intangibles

Breeding true champions is really about developing character and all the intangibles the great athletes possess. Players with character are better performers when the game is on the line because they never cheat themselves or their teammates. They are always giving 100%, whether in practice or a game, and they have their teammates' energy pulling for them. So they trust themselves more, and their teammates trust them too. They soon develop more confidence and skill to perform in tough situations.

Kevin Towers, general manager for the San Diego Padres, discusses the importance of intangibles such as instincts, desire, and drive: "Tony Gwynn's that way; he wants the bat in his hand when the game's on the line. Trevor Hoffman's the guy who wants to be in there with the bases loaded and a 3-2 count; he knows he has to throw a strike. Not everybody's like that. I'm sure that Rick Barry was the guy that wanted to be shooting the free throw with the game on the line, Michael Jordan wants the ball in his hands, Joe Montana was a guy that with two minutes left, would rather be in that part of the game with the game on the line than the start of the first quarter. Those guys are hard to find. When you find those types of guys, you build your organization around them."

Having character gives a player confidence. For example, his work ethic removes doubts that he was outworked by his opponents. Also, because he has integrity and his teammates know they can count on him, they are pulling for him and giving him their energy. With this kind of confidence, players are poised to win. They are able to handle obstacles that come their way, and when things get tough, they have the mental toughness to get through it. A player may prepare for a scenario that never occurs, but he's not nervous because he knows he is prepared for anything.

Carroll Land at Point Loma Nazarene knows there's only one way to maximize someone's ability. He explains: "We expect a very, very strong work ethic. The teams that are good for the most part have great work ethic. A lot of kids are willing to work hard but don't know how, so you have an expectation of a strong work ethic, but you have to help individuals learn how to do that. And I believe that most kids want to work hard, because they do believe that it's going to make them better."

When players learn to work hard, and work hard with their teammates, they build bonds between each other as well as discipline and self-confidence. Pat Murphy, head coach at Arizona State University, knows this well. "[To develop team unity] we work the heck out of them. They respond. It's like you never met anybody that's been through basic training that doesn't have a common bond because they work so damn hard. I think that's a real key."

Build Their Entire Lives

Murphy pushes his players to excel on and off the field. He believes if they are good citizens, they'll be better teammates and they'll learn to trust one another. "[My philosophy is to use] the role of a coach first to be a teacher, and to help develop young people as people, as athletes, as competitors, as citizens," Murphy says.

One of the ways coaches help players grow as individuals is through community projects. Jim Dietz, long-time head coach at San Diego State University, did a lot of work with his players off the field, which influenced his coaching techniques on the field as well. "We do a lot of things like work projects and things in the community. I let the players take a leadership role and I watch who the leaders are and who the followers are. It's amazing what you find out. You will find more out about somebody there than you will in a baseball game, because what you will find there will carry over to the game. Some kids can really step up and handle pressure and some kids, probably because of how they were brought up as youngsters, never will handle much pressure in their lives. It's just human nature."

Gamers and Fox-Hole Guys

Davey Johnson, 1997 American League Manager of the Year for the Baltimore Orioles, wants players that he can count on when the heat is on. He's not so much looking for guys who just hit the long ball, but guys who have some ability and also integrity.

He explains: "You can win with great talent, or you can win with mediocre talent that has a lot of great drive, intestinal fortitude. If you get that kind of mix, the gamers, guys that don't have great talent, but give you everything they got, those are the kind of guys I call foxhole guys. They won't fall asleep. They're better than the great talented guys that would fall asleep. There have been a lot of times when I passed on really good talent because I didn't think he had the makeup to give me all he had. And if you have great talent and you're afraid to really give it all you got, you're not going to win. You're better off with a foxhole guy that will grind it out, day in and day out. You just have to be able to decide when you judge that talent. It's important, if you want to have a team that wins and has chemistry. That means they have to have heart, they have to care. That's important. That's probably the biggest thing."

Gamers not only get the most out of their own ability but also inspire others to do the same. In the locker room before South Africa's huge victory over the Netherlands in the 2000 Olympics, the author discussed the need for one guy to step forward, one guy to lead, to say, "Come on, climb on – I'll take us there." South Africa found that guy, or rather those guys, in Tim Harrell's complete game victory and Ian Holness going four-for-four with 12 total bases, including the game-winning home run in the tenth inning. Their energy, determination, and confidence inspired an entire team.

Terry Francona, former manager of the Philadelphia Phillies, says his idea of a gamer is exemplified by Scott Rolen: "For me, he's about as solid as you can get. Talent-wise he's very, very good. Other than that, when he doesn't hit, he's always trying to find a way to win. He's a great base runner. He's a good defensive player. He hustles, he's conscientious, and he gives you everything he has every day to try to win. That's about perfect."

One way to sum up the character of a "gamer," the ideal player, is to describe his attitude. He's the guy that Francona says "gives you everything he has every day to try to win." His attitude displays his character—how bad he wants it, how much he's willing to sacrifice to get it, and what kind of integrity he has. A player with an unstoppable determination to be the best he can be helps himself and his teammates, while inspiring others.

Instill Discipline

To be the best they can be, players know it takes hard work and self-discipline. However, with so many distractions they are not always very disciplined and/or efficient with their time.

Tom Kelly, long-time manager of the Minnesota Twins (world champions in 1987 and 1991), discusses the need for discipline: "Everybody likes a little discipline in their life. Show up on time, be responsible for your actions. I don't think anybody likes being scolded or anything of that nature, but to a certain extent we all like to have rules to follow or a code to speak, of what we're going to do, on how we're going to handle ourselves."

Discipline is critical for growth. Players have to carry themselves a certain way depending on which team they are on. The Los Angeles Dodgers and Charlie Blaney, long-time director of player personnel, feel strongly about this: "We have a certain discipline. We don't tolerate throwing helmets or breaking bats or carrying on that's not professional when they strike out. When a player reads in *Baseball America* that he's one of the top 10 prospects and then he starts acting like he's arrived, then we address that. So, just like a family who is there every day, you can sense when players are getting a big head or when they are down in the dumps. That is why it is so important to have a caring and sensitive coaching staff who realize theirs' is not a nine to five job. Perhaps a player needs to be taken out for lunch. Or maybe he needs a pat on the back or a kick in the rear. It's a people reaction. No set guidelines, rules or regulations exist in this case. It's a human being relationship that we emphasize."

One of the most important outcomes of disciplinary action is that the player and the team get better for it. If someone makes a mistake and learns from it, then discipline is corrective rather than punitive.

Tom Trebelhorn, former manager of the Milwaukee Brewers and the Chicago Cubs, noted this difference: "Discipline is more of a team message. You have to confront individual actions for the sake of the other 24 players. That person is going to be held accountable for behavior or negligence or whatever it might be that needs the confrontation. But I try to distance myself from the individually punitive philosophy to a corrective one. The other 24 are going to see me yell at one player, confront that player, deal with that player. I've got nothing personal against that particular player, but I've got to do this. That's the way it is, he's just one out of 25 who has to be disciplined so that the others don't have to be. It's a message you have to send to the whole club. Most guys don't really mean to do things that force discipline, they just make mistakes."

Andy Lopez instills discipline by holding teammates accountable for each other, in more ways than one: "If a player is late to practice, he'll stand with me in the middle of the field while his teammates run. They'll get punished for his tardiness. This accomplishes two things: one, that player makes sure he's not late anymore, and two, he feels some guilt that they're running in place of him. In a strange way, there's some camaraderie that starts to develop there. Players are accountable for each other, so it works both ways." Do the players get bitter? "The first time they won't. They'll get after each other a bit, but if it happens three times in three weeks, I'll guarantee you there's a problem. But, then we've got a bigger problem on our hands. It's what's going on in a player's life, so slowly you'll see that start to separate itself."

Help Each Other Become Disciplined

Self-discipline is crucial to achieving individual success, and in turn, team success. Without self-discipline, players won't be accountable for their actions, and coaches won't know if they can rely on them. So, coaches try hard to instill discipline in their players. However, a lot of the discipline needs to be done by their own teammates.

Lopez requires his players to enact the discipline on each other: "We have two rules in the program: be on time and do things right. Doing things right is paying attention to everything going on in your world every day. For example, if you walk into the clubhouse and you're putting on soccer socks and everyone else is putting on stirrups, you know soccer socks are not right. If someone shows up with soccer socks, we make sure we let everybody know this is not right. You'll learn what doing things right every day means. It's neat for me, because you see a real spurt of growth when someone finally figures out what doing things right means. In other words, it's right to go to class, it's right to dress proper on a road trip. It's right to ask questions if you're not sure. It's wrong to assume. It's an everyday growth. For example, it's right to knock or check with the secretary before you come into the coach's office because he could be in a meeting or something. It's neat to see an older guy show the younger guys what's right and wrong."

If teammates are conscientious, and monitor each other, then the coach can do more coaching and motivating. Larry Dierker, while managing for the Houston Astros, had teams that disciplined themselves. He explains how he handles discipline: "I don't have to handle it much at all, because I've got players like Biggio, Bagwell, Alou, Reynolds and Hampton. Some of our name players, [such as] Derek Bell, go about their business in a very professional way. When you have your front-line players who do that, there's not much discipline required."

Being professional is enacting self-discipline, which is not an easy task. A player has to watch closely what he says, how he carries himself, how he treats his teammates, and, even how he treats his parents. The idea is to act with integrity in every way.

Legendary manager Sparky Anderson believes that there is much more to developing champions than just what is between the lines. He says, "I think the great coaches are the guys who are able to take great talent and make them great professionals."

Another legendary manager, Gene Mauch of the California Angels, felt strongly that the players had to help each other with discipline: "For the most part, you have a set of rules and the players discipline themselves. As far as fines are concerned, they laugh at a [couple] hundred or thousand dollar fine. When you're blessed with two or three key people on a team, they'll incorporate their own discipline on one another. The great clubs like the Dodgers had in Brooklyn, they policed one another. You set down rules, then the players discipline themselves, they fine themselves."

Bob Todd, head coach at Ohio State, also emphasizes this point. Todd says, "Players have to discipline themselves. You can say all you want about a hard-nosed coach, but the players have to buy into the system that we are going to do everything we possibly can, every minute, every day—that we are here to make ourselves the best people we can be. That means the best student, the best person, the best baseball player, and if they'll continue to do that...like I said, it's a life. It's not something you turn off and on like a faucet. It's something that permeates on the field and is also there off the field."

The players are able to push and monitor each other better than the coach because for one thing, they spend a lot more time around each other. The players see each other on and off the field. They can do much more to influence their teammates, and thus have a lot to do with whether they and each other continually strive for excellence.

Francona adds, "One thing I feel very strongly about is the players policing themselves. They do a good job. I've got some veterans who understand how I feel, and I think they agree with it, and they keep guys in line. I'll handle the bigger things, but with the little things the players police themselves."

Being able to depend on front line guys to keep the others in line and help monitor the team is such a big factor. Getting a couple of the key players to lead by example, and give a stern look to anyone who doesn't follow suit, is immensely beneficial. Gary Adams, head coach at UCLA, illustrates: "One of the biggest things I use is peer pressure. I make them feel that they would be letting their teammates down if they ever did anything that went against the rules we have in the Sphere (see Chapter 2). They don't want to look bad in front of their teammates. Sometimes it's macho to speak up against the coach or to do something against the coach. But it's not macho to do something against teammates and hurt the team. So I use the team."

Self-Motivated

The value of self-motivation is seen when you look at anyone who has accomplished anything great. Successful men have a fire burning within that not only propels them to succeed, but motivates others also. If a team has players who will go out and hit in the cage in the middle of winter while there is snow on the ground, they will motivate others.

Terry Collins, former manager of the Anaheim Angels, wants the guys to learn to manage themselves. "[To build a championship team,] I'd find those guys who are self-motivated and guys who are willing to sacrifice their numbers for the good of the team. That's what I consider a winning-type player. You certainly want to find guys who can do things and who have skills. But you want to find the guys who manage themselves. You give them direction and turn them loose. Those are the kind of players you win with."

When players learn to manage themselves and be accountable, then they not only improve on and off the field, but they will also gain the respect of their teammates. That is a trait of many championship teams.

Make Them Believe They Are Greater Than They Are

All players have greatness within them. Maybe their greatness lies in the fact that they can go from sitting on the bench for three weeks to getting the game-winning hit in the bottom of the thirteenth. Maybe it's that they can pitch once every five days and motivate their teammates the other days. Perhaps their greatness comes from hitting jacks (home runs).

Whatever that greatness is, great coaches first teach their players to recognize their potential, then help them achieve it. The famous philosopher Goethe said, "When we treat man as he is, we make him worse than he is; when we treat him as if he already were what he potentially could be, we make him what he should be."[1] The championship coach stretches his players' confidence and inspires them to fulfill their potential.

Chuck Cottier, former expansion manager for the Seattle Mariners, had to work really hard at getting his players to believe in themselves. He explains, "The most important thing for me with an expansion team was to let these guys play so that they felt like they were major league players, so they believed in themselves. [With] a veteran club you might pinch-hit in key situations, you might make a pitching change a little bit earlier, but when you have young players and you're trying to prove to them that they're major league players, there are certain times when you have to let them go a little bit further, to get them over the hump."

When players start believing in themselves, focusing on the pursuit of excellence, and trying to be the best they can be, there will be a few individuals who achieve far beyond what anyone had expected. This is the end result of taking everything one step at a time. Having an intense work ethic, integrity, self-discipline, confidence, and self-motivation leads to one becoming a true team player. When you develop guys who will encourage each other to raise the bar and play like champions, great things can happen.

The championship coach continually expects his players to be greater tomorrow than they were today. The reason he challenges his players to put in that extra effort is so they can achieve more than anyone expected of them.

Pat Murphy describes his philosophy by saying, "One of our goals is obviously to become better players and citizens. Another is to go where you haven't gone before, do some things that you haven't done before. I believe that we do not know what our best is. I don't like players to put limits on themselves as to how good they can be. Sometimes they do."

When players don't put limits on themselves, they have the chance to become much more than they have ever been. The great coaches find ways to make that happen, or allow it to happen. They provide an environment where players can rise up to their potential.

Tom Trebelhorn says that's necessary to reach the pinnacle in the sport: "Winning a championship takes all the players who you're counting on to be productive, up to the level that you expect, and a couple of players who you didn't count on having really quality years. Most clubs that win have a player who comes out of nowhere. Not only do the players who they were counting on do fine, but also some pitcher comes out and wins 15 or 16 games they didn't count on, or some position player they didn't count on ends up hitting .280 with 91 RBI's. You have to have good productivity from your quality players and somehow in some areas, with overachievers or surprise achievers, have somebody who was not counted upon do really well. You can't really have a breakdown of your key productive players. They have to come through and somebody else has to step forward who pleasantly surprises you. And that happens every year."

Principle #1
Build Individual Champions

Baseball is an individual sport played in a team format, with plenty of failure built into the game. For this reason, it is an ideal sport to examine and to use as a reference for how to overcome adversity in athletics, and how to bring individuals together as a team.

To achieve that teamwork, individual champions need to be developed—players with mental toughness, integrity, perseverance, and courage. Then they can be counted on when the tough times come. To handle the adversity takes a person with character, resilience, and discipline.

When the coach knows he has players with character, then he has options. He knows they are more likely to buy into the plan (i.e., the covenant), and the players will be able to reap the great results of teamwork. And if they have some fortitude, some mental toughness, then he knows they will not quit on him. Therefore, he will have a chance to make his team more than the sum of the parts, because he'll have individual champions who "overachieve."

Not only is it a common element of championship teams to have at least one guy who has a better-than-expected season, but also it is possibly the greatest compliment a player can give his coach—that he inspired him and somehow compelled him to reach beyond what many, including himself, thought he could do.

CHAPTER 2

Form a Covenant

"I have a mission statement and a covenant that every player signs. Our mission statement is: *Excellence both on and off the field.* You should have a mission statement that reflects your values. Your covenant should be the same way. Every team should have a covenant. That way your players will know what's expected of them. We take our covenant very seriously."

> — Skip Bertman
> Five-time NCAA Division I national champion,
> Louisiana State University

In discussing their philosophy, managers and coaches voiced a common theme: have a plan that is clearly laid out, make sure everyone knows the big goal, and get everyone to buy into the process of achieving that goal. This theme also encompasses making each player accountable for his actions, instilling pride in one's self and the team, and having faith in the system and each other.

Forming a covenant is a way of communicating the team philosophy. It consists of clearly defining the team's ideals and role of each person, developing teamwork, and laying a foundation for success. It is comparable to a mission statement in form, but goes into more detail, describing the team's goals and core values, and the mode of achieving those goals.

World champion basketball coach Pat Riley, a master motivator, gets his teams to commit to giving 100% effort every day, and believe in themselves. He has what he calls a "core covenant," which is described as follows:

The Constructive Covenant

...binds people together,
...creates an equal footing,
...helps people shoulder their own responsibilities,
...prescribes terms for the help and support of others,
...and creates a foundation for teamwork.

> — Pat Riley

Riley's values set the framework for his covenant. He says, "The most profound core covenant I know of, the Declaration of Independence, reverberates with these words: 'We hold these truths to be self-evident, that all men are created equal, that they are endowed by their creator with certain unalienable Rights.' Every team that wants to move toward significance and greatness has to decide what truths it will hold to be self-evident and to get those values circulating throughout the organization," Riley explains.[1]

Baseball is a game with so much adversity that without a clear vision of where they want to be and how to get there, a team can easily be sidetracked. A covenant, or plan of attack, which describes the physical and mental processes needed to fulfill their vision, gives them the focus to overcome challenges. Without clearly defined values, goals, and modes of operation, players will take different paths—it is like each person having his own set of blueprints. With this kind of indifference toward the team, they may venture off the team's path and get caught in negatives such as selfishness, distrust, or lack of faith.

Without a framework for making minute-to-minute decisions, what a player becomes is less than what he could be, and thus, he will not be able to elevate his teammates the way he could. A good covenant helps players be focused and confident.

Skip Bertman's national championship teams started every year with a covenant. His players and coaches all agreed upon and signed a covenant before each season. "To become champions you have to build the players' entire lives. That's why I start with a very clear and very strong mission statement that applies to my players' lives. Every team should have one. Our mission statement is: *Excellence both on and off the field.*" Bertman describes excellence as, "a continuous, relentless, never-ending commitment to improve; the gradual result of always trying to get better."

The covenant Bertman's players at LSU sign discusses the importance of academics, a proper moral environment (on and off the field), and the importance of teamwork, cooperation, and friendship. It also details items such as trust, work ethic, and the team motto. Part of his covenant is that good enough never is—it's about players and coaches putting forth their absolute best effort, every day.

Just above the player's signature Bertman's covenant reads, "I promise to play as well as I can every day, to represent my school, my family, and my maker with 110% effort; to play like a champion." By signing the covenant, each player and coach agrees that he will do his best to uphold the values within. It is a two-way agreement that solidifies the team. Simply by signing the agreement, the players and coaches share a bond, and it expresses their strong commitment.

Putting the Covenant Into a Visual Image

Covenants come in all different forms. Some are unwritten, some are written, and some have accompanying pictures. Those championship coaches with unwritten covenants still relay the message effectively. They tell their players all year long what is expected of them, and are very clear about their responsibilities and team goals. Players know how they are supposed to act, even though it is not written out.

Some coaches have taken it a step further and put the covenant into a visual image. One of the greatest coaches of all time, basketball legend John Wooden, developed the Pyramid of Success at UCLA to give his players a foundation for living and basis for action. Wooden's Pyramid offers a set of positive choices on the path to success.

Gary Adams, head baseball coach at UCLA, worked alongside Wooden and came up with the Sphere of Commitment. Like the Pyramid, it's a tangible document that the players can look at, study, and use to draw them in a common direction. It is something to bring them together as a team—a visual they can put on their wall and point to when questions arise.

Adams explains, "My philosophy is shown by the Sphere of Commitment. There's so much more to coaching than just winning and having a national championship. That'd be nice to have, and that's my quest, but just because you don't get that doesn't mean you failed in all the other just as important areas, areas that are on the Sphere of Commitment. I feel good about the guys who played for me and became doctors, lawyers, and teachers. I don't care if they're garbage men, if they've got good character and if I've imparted some knowledge to help them. To me, they're winners. You don't have to have a trophy to be a winner."

Spiritual Foundation

The heart of a championship covenant is often a spiritual foundation. A player can sign the covenant and want to do all the things in the covenant, but without inner strength, it is impossible to accomplish anything great. Great accomplishments derive from great adversity. To withstand the adversity, a player needs a way to circumvent the challenges that arise.

A spiritual foundation is important armor against adversity. It is an inner focus (the Chinese call it Chi), which harnesses personal energy, energy from teammates, and energy from the environment. It synergizes the link between body and spirit, enhancing inner focus during competition.

Getting "centered" is an important part of achieving one's potential as an individual and as a team. Especially in a sport that is often regarded as 80 –90 percent mental, having an inner focus is vital. A strong spiritual foundation enhances inner focus and enables the nervous system to remain calm in pressure-packed situations, and, in turn, gives one the ability to play well amidst chaos.

For Bob Todd, spirituality is his foundation. It governs his personal life, and baseball is no different. He explains, "The majority of my philosophy on life and baseball revolves around religion and a belief in God. No stealing, no lying, no cheating—there's a spiritual or biblical background to it. I really believe that coaches should harp on quality of life."

THE SPHERE OF COMMITMENT OF THE UCLA COACH

© Gary Adams

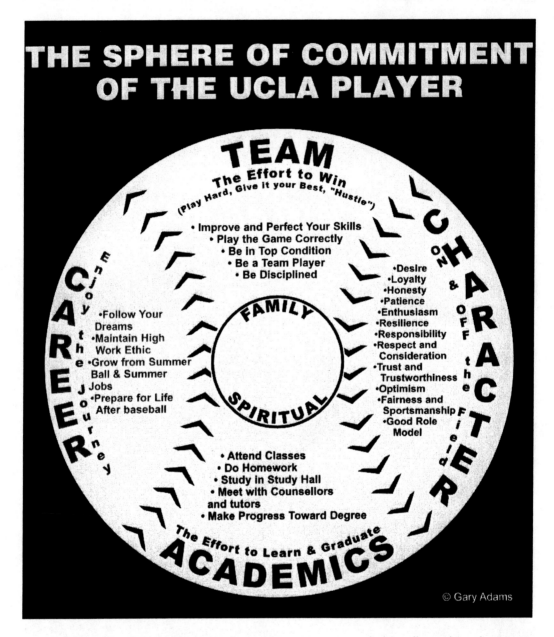

THE SPHERE OF COMMITMENT OF THE UCLA PLAYER

TEAM
The Effort to Win
(Play Hard, Give it your Best, "Hustle")

• Improve and Perfect Your Skills
• Play the Game Correctly
• Be in Top Condition
• Be a Team Player
• Be Disciplined

FAMILY

SPIRITUAL

CHARACTER
On & Off the Field

•Desire
•Loyalty
•Honesty
•Patience
•Enthusiasm
•Resilience
•Responsibility
•Respect and
 Consideration
•Trust and
 Trustworthiness
•Optimism
•Fairness and
 Sportsmanship
•Good Role
 Model

CAREER
Enjoy the Journey

•Follow Your
 Dreams
•Maintain High
 Work Ethic
•Grow from Summer
 Ball & Summer
 Jobs
•Prepare for Life
 After baseball

• Attend Classes
• Do Homework
• Study in Study Hall
• Meet with Counsellors
  and tutors
• Make Progress Toward Degree

The Effort to Learn & Graduate
ACADEMICS

© Gary Adams

Todd's spiritual foundation anchors his covenant, and this allows his players to know where he is coming from and what he values. If a coach has deep-rooted values to live his life a certain way, then his team should know that, and he should coach that way. Otherwise he will continually run into conflicts. Todd would not be living true to his values if he allowed contradictions to them on his own team.

Jerry Kindall elaborates, "When I became a coach, I decided the way to bring my team together was to expect a higher standard of conduct from them than other teams have. My own lifestyle is based on scriptural principles. I wasn't trying to impose my spiritual beliefs on my players but what I am I can't deny."

A spiritual foundation connects the mind, body, and spirit. It is very powerful to line up those three areas because when they are in sync, a synergy develops that helps deal with the adversity in life and in baseball. It is not about religion. It is about tapping the inner power that everyone has, that elevates athletes to incredible accomplishments.

Todd explains, "You've got to start with a religious, spiritual, or belief in God somewhere, no matter how you believe in Him. I don't care whether you're Muslim, Baptist, or Catholic, it doesn't matter. You've got to have a spiritual belief somewhere, and that foundation will dictate your lifestyle and dictate your beliefs to everybody; you can't be afraid to expound those to your team. You can't force your beliefs on players, but you've got to let them know where you're coming from or you end up confusing your players. The less confused they are about where you're coming from, the better off you are. Nothing comes easy.

"If you've got a belief in God and you believe in what you're doing and you work hard at it, sooner or later something good is going to come of it. People who say that's too tough or don't want to do it are not going to have [the same kind of] success that the most successful people do," Todd continues.

Make Life Congruent

The core covenant helps players focus and create inner strength. It also helps them attain synergy with their teammates in mind, body, and spirit, keeping them congruent (i.e., in harmony). It forces players to face up to their values. If a team has players with integrity, then their actions will coincide with their values, and this is a position of strength. The core covenant puts into writing these values, which serve as guidelines for achieving success. It informs players of the team's values and instructs them on how to behave in order to act in accordance with their beliefs.

Congruence is also about players linking themselves with personal values, with teammates, and with the Creator, whomever they deem that to be. Prayer is one possible way to accomplish this. Praying is powerful, as it can release stress and increase faith. When people stop worrying and start trusting that things will work out, then they are in a position of power. They stop battling themselves, and, in the end, that is the ultimate battle. A spiritual foundation is a stronghold for winning the battle with oneself.

Bob Todd knows that good teamwork starts with individuals who are true to themselves and their values: "There's a certain philosophy I've got on what it takes to compete. The two most important things you've got are your spiritual beliefs and then your family, and out of that comes the team."

When a team is congruent with its core values, it moves toward realms beyond the ordinary. Players trust each other. Without congruence toward one's values and the values of the team, doubt creeps in and so does distrust. Cognitive dissonance is a psychological term that may help explain incongruence. It is when one's beliefs and actions do not line up. For example, when a talented player is not playing well, he knows he is a good player, but his actions are not showing it. So, mentally he has to either switch his beliefs (to believing he is not talented), or find an outside reason as to why he is not performing well. He has to blame it on something or someone else. Maybe he's just in a slump, which is a normal part of baseball. Or maybe the guy in front of him is continually making the third out of the inning and forcing him to lead off. It is not his fault (it's the fault of the batter in front of him). Thus, cognitive dissonance can cause dissension when players start blaming others. This stems from a lack of trust.

When players lose faith in themselves, they create cognitive dissonance. Maybe they do not quite trust their abilities because they have not been working as hard as they should. Their conflicting beliefs (they believe they are a great player, but they are not exerting the effort they know they should be), cause incongruence, which, in turn, may cause conflict.

Another example of cognitive dissonance can be seen when a player has values on how to carry himself and on what is right and wrong, yet his actions do not reflect those values. This misalignment of beliefs and actions robs him of his power. Either way it's explained, when one's actions don't reflect one's core beliefs, the person cannot expect the greatness that lies within to be freely expressed.

Get a Commitment

When there's conflict, adversity, and/or disarray, players and teams either have some strong belief to fall back on or they fall apart. The team's covenant helps hold them together. The covenant may consist of values such as committing to the team and the team's goals, continually improving as a player, studying the game, being personally accountable, etc.

Commitment to a purpose, a clearly defined purpose outlined in the covenant, gives players strength when things are tough. They may commit to having integrity and faith—faith in their maker, their team, and themselves. They may have a commitment to taking pride in their character, their actions, and their team.

Bob Bennett starts every year with a commitment from his players: "The first thing is to get people to commit to a goal. You present your goal and recruit people who have the same goal. Once you've established that commitment, then your job as a coach is to say, 'we have to do these things in order to build a team, and I'm going to hold you to it. You promised me at the beginning of the season that's what you wanted, and now it's my job to make sure you hold up to your promise.'"

When players have a common goal, a clear plan to accomplish that goal, and a belief in the goal, great things can happen. When one of those three things does not happen, it is very difficult to win. The clear plan is outlined in the covenant.

At Mississippi State, the players know what is expected of them when they arrive, as head coach Ron Polk explains: "We talk a lot to our ball club about what commitment needs to be made at Mississippi State in baseball, academically, and how they handle themselves on and off the field. I think the thing most people equate Mississippi State with is kids who play hard and have a lot of character and class.

"We have certain rules and regulations about shining their shoes before ball games, their haircut, how long their sideburns can be, how neat the mustaches may be, how they run on and off the field, and how they go to first base on a base on balls. It's a team game, but, at the same time, an individual game. We have team concepts we definitely value which include no cussing, no bad words, treat the other team with great respect, but play hard and try to beat them."

Jerry Kindall discusses the commitment he expected from his players at Arizona: "With the agreement of my assistant coaches, we put in no profanity, no swearing, respect your opponents, that kind of thing. Respect the umpires. Dress neatly. We had a hair rule and we had a mustache rule, but the players agreed to that. They saw that there was a purpose to all come together in a common way. So, although they don't like to wear ties and they don't like to shave every day… they had to be clean-shaven when we appeared together on the road or boarded a plane."

The team policy at Arizona was the basis for how they acted. When Kindall spoke to his players, they knew he was being honest, doing the best he could to make the team the best it could be. They knew the team policy, and they watched him carefully to see if he followed up on it. He did. Kindall explains, "There are times when I'll address the team, I'll say this is what I think is right. They may not agree altogether, but I want them to understand that it does come from a basis of fact and that it works for me.

"The other things that prevail are having an understanding of the team goals and what the coaches are trying to do and their ability or willingness to tie into those goals. I don't ask my players to always agree with me in what I'm doing or how I'm putting in the lineup or my strategy, but I do ask them to try to understand that we are all working together for the common good, to make our team successful."

Respect the Team

When players put the team above themselves, it allows everyone to come out ahead. If everyone is pulling in the same direction, that puts them in a position for everyone to excel. Putting the team first means respecting the covenant and the values it entails. Players should respect themselves enough to not let their conflicts with a teammate take away from the team goals. Players should learn that disrespecting others robs themselves of power. Showing disrespect is a way of emitting negative energy, and that negativity will be returned.

Letting individual differences interfere with the focus of the team drags all the other players into the problem. Then it becomes everyone else's problem. Players soon realize that personalities will not always get along, but there has to be some respect to put the team first for the greater good of everyone. Because there can be no World Series MVP without the help of his teammates to make it to the World Series.

Respect the Game

Respecting the game is a continuation of respecting oneself and others. Respecting the game is not only about playing hard and playing to win, but also knowing how tough the game is, and how it can really knock a player down if he is not careful.

Tom Kelly demands his players' respect, for the game and each other. He explains, "I don't like to look over their shoulders, I like to let them play. I like them to respect the game first. The game deserves respect. If you don't have a respect for it, the game will beat you up.

"Play the game the right way, win or lose. You run the ball out, hustle to your position, and entertain the people that pay a lot of money to come see these games. If somebody's going to disrespect the game or disrespect a fan, or treat the game wrongly, then they're going to have problems. I'm not going to put up with it. I think we put those cards out on the table, and we go forward from there, that way I don't have any problems."

Team Leaders Are the Catalyst

An essential ingredient in any championship team is having players who not only lead by example, but also get others to follow their example. They push the other players to have the respect and integrity outlined in the covenant. Championship coaches repeat this idea: a great team has players who are leaders, who push and police the others to do what's best for the team—leaders who enforce the covenant, who know how to play, and respect the game.

Kelly explains, "One thing that's helped here is that I've had very talented players that came to play the game, and set a precedent that this is how you do it. Within that, you know I had Hrbek, Gaetti, Puckett, Molitor, and Jack Morris, people that know how to play the game, and play it at a high level. They showed the others that this is how it's done. You approach the game this way, and that's it, there's no other way."

A coach or manager can be the greatest motivator, the greatest game manager, and the most knowledgeable coach, but without a few players who can also lead, the road to success can be a long one. Players who understand the team concept and work hard toward that and inspire their teammates to do the same are really the cog that makes the machine run at full capacity.

"I've been lucky that way to have these kinds of people come in the clubhouse and play here. They set the tone and the others follow. If somebody has a problem with that, then they're going to come in here and see me and they're going to be sitting by me, because they're not going to be playing, because they're not respecting the game," Kelly explains.

Integrity

At the heart of a solid covenant is integrity. If players have integrity, there's a higher level of trust, and that type of environment fosters teamwork. When players trust each other, it elevates the synergy of their team. Distrust zaps energy to where players begin to put in only enough work to get the job done, and they are always on the lookout for someone else who is doing the same. The problem is that distrust turns into a vicious cycle, where the players put out less and less effort, and put in more and more distrust and individual promotion.

You can count on players with integrity to be leaders on and off the field, setting the example, doing things right. Bob Todd explains his view on integrity in players: "If a kid that comes into your program doesn't have character, he probably isn't going to survive. If he steals, cheats, and lies, then that's what he's going to do to his teammates, and that's really what he's going to do to himself when it comes down to it."

Having integrity is like having a solid cornerstone for success in any field, and baseball is no different. The idea is to develop a place where the athlete can feel good about himself and know he's being true to his values, and feel his actions line up with his deep beliefs. Players with a solid foundation of integrity know their place in the world, their higher purpose. They are confident in who they are, and how they fit in with their teammates and everyone else.

When it comes down to it, they are more comfortable with themselves, and they are able to stand alone because they've got a hundred other people backing them up. This helps them when they are the one who has to throw *that* strike, hit *that* pitch, or field *that* ball. This is important when it's just the player versus the game.

Bob Todd explains how integrity is important for facing those situations when the player needs to make a play: "*Mano y mano*, one-on-one on a field in competitive battle. It's the hitter versus the pitcher. It's the shortstop versus the ground ball, and that defensive player has to have that characteristic and that belief that he's going to do it and not blame somebody else. It's about being your best not only in baseball but socially, in the classroom, with your relationships, your family, your girlfriend, and on the baseball field. If you're successful in all areas, you are going to be a better baseball player; you make them believe that."

Having integrity helps players believe in themselves, because the heart of integrity is helping others, which is not only the right thing to do, but it also bears good fruits and brings confidence.

"Character is not something you turn on and off like a water fountain. It's something you live. It's a lifestyle. People can't say, 'I am going to cheat this person because I don't like him and I like this person so I am not going to cheat him.' That's not character, that's seeing what you can get away with. What you have to do is find people that have the belief that everything you do in life, you are going to try to do the very best you can," Todd explains.

When a player knows a teammate has that kind of attitude, that they will do their very best in everything they do, and do what is right, then they will develop a high degree of trust in that player, belief in that player, and, in the end, achieve great synergy with that player.

Teamwork and Trust

Bob Bennett starts the season explaining to his players how important teamwork and trust is on his team: "We draw a little circle on the board, and it has nothing in it. We say that's the beginning of our team. The first day you make any kind of gesture toward playing or practicing, you put something into that circle. If you put mistrust in it then that's part of our team. If you put trust in it, that becomes part of our team. If you put laziness in it, that becomes part of our team. It's our job to get rid of all of the negatives and make sure that circle is filled with positives. When it's filled with positives, you have a great ball club."

Skip Bertman does something similar using a crystal ball as a symbol of team trust. He says that the actions of each member of the team go into that ball. (Each player receives one, plus there's a big one in the office.) Everything a player does becomes part of the team, whether it's showing love, respecting others, or behaving wrongly—it all goes in. If someone drops the ball with a serious incident of mistrust, then it can never be put back together like it was. In other words, it shatters.

Trust is so crucial to develop because it provides an environment where players are not afraid to take risks, where they're not afraid to disagree or step up and say, "You're not pulling your share of the load, you've got to get going." Trust allows players to speak out honestly without feeling that others will take it the wrong way. Bertman says that trust is something someone either has or does not have—it's all or nothing. Trust is like character, it's not something that can be switched on and off.

Mike Hargrove explains the importance of trust: "I like to use an old truism, 'honesty is the best policy.' I think with today's athletes, if they can trust you and know that you're going to tell them the truth, no matter what the circumstances, then from that base there are different directions that you can take people."

Personal Development

Success in baseball takes total focus on the field and balance in the rest of life: in resting and relaxing, in stimulating the mind for self-improvement, in knowing one's place in the world. When players lack perspective, they lose their sense of being part of something larger than themselves. An effective covenant, therefore, may stress personal development as well as the application of their talent. It's learning one's place in the world and working toward improving that.

For Jim Dietz, forming a team was about recruiting good people and bringing together all the pieces of life. Dietz's coaching taught about life, and focused on personal development as a means toward playing better baseball: "We don't always recruit the best athletes, we try to recruit the best kids—so that's a little bit of a different approach. We live together for six to seven months, so we've got to have good people who are low maintenance, because we don't have a lot of time for high maintenance people.

"Our approach is pretty upright and simple. There are no gimmicks, no videos or motivational talks. We just know what we have to do. We try to do some things together; some of the guys like to fish or hunt so we'll go and do that. We do a lot of things in terms of work. We adopt some schools, we adopt a couple of freeways, we do a lot of things in the community. And I think that's the reason the donor donated all the money for this stadium, because of this community-oriented approach.

"I think that's the best way to approach it because if you approach athletics just from a winning standpoint—everything's win, win, win—then you are going to lose a lot more than you're going to win. It's better to approach it from students and future development and human beings and getting along and trying to help one another.

"We hold people responsible, and if somebody makes a bad decision and somebody else knew a bad decision was being made and didn't intervene, then we would hold that person just as responsible. This is because he should help a teammate or he should help somebody else. So, our approach is probably a lot different than a lot of places," Dietz explains.

Pat Murphy sees his most important role as assisting his players' personal development. "My main role is that of a teacher, to teach the right things in life." Murphy pushes his players hard and expects a lot from them. But, like Jim Dietz, he encourages his players to become involved in their community: "We have a lot of team meetings during which the players talk about how they feel. We work very hard during practice, we do a lot of team things in the off-season, whether it is visiting a church and helping clean their schoolyard, or visiting elementary schools. We do a lot off the field to help the players grow as people."

Professional teams have the same philosophy in that regard, as Charlie Blaney explains: "We look at our responsibility to help the player be a complete Dodger player, on and off the field. Therefore, we help teach them how to dress properly, be on time, talk to the media, plan for life after baseball, handle the cheering, and handle the booing. We teach them how to handle the gals that are going to chase after them, how to say no to drugs and alcohol and steroids—all of these things we feel are our responsibility in helping the young men."

Faith

Growing and developing as individuals and as a team takes faith. It takes faith in oneself, one's teammates, and one's coach. Faith is so important because it allows visualization to be more concrete, and it develops trust in teammates. A team must have faith that when the going gets tough, they will be able to handle it. When adversity comes, a team with faith will not deviate from the things it needs to do to be successful.

If a player believes that he will be able to manage anything that comes his way, but doesn't trust that his teammates can do the same, then that player will be critical of others and put chinks in the armor of team synergy. Faith comes through a player knowing his teammates, working hard, and going through tough times together to comprehend the fact that his teammates will stick with him. When a team has faith and trust in each other, great things can happen.

Having trust allows individuals to take risks on the field because they are secure in the knowledge that their teammates will support them no matter what. Faith built on trust also relieves the burden of one individual ever taking the responsibility (or blame) for a team's losses. Likewise, one player cannot claim to be the sole reason for the team's success.

Believing that players can acquire, as the season progresses, the necessary attributes for themselves and the team to fulfill their dream is also important. On paper a team may have four quality starters, but without a fifth starter, it's hard for players to visualize winning it all. Or maybe a team doesn't seem to have the leaders who sustain momentum when the times are tough. But, with faith that these things will come, it has a chance to happen. A quality fifth starter will step up, and so will the leaders. Players need to have faith that everyone on the team will come through when called upon, and for this, they need to be accountable to do what it takes to get there.

Dusty Baker, manager of the San Francisco Giants, played for Tommy Lasorda with the Los Angeles Dodgers. He enjoyed playing for Lasorda; one reason was Lasorda's belief in his players and the team: "Tommy had faith. That was the one thing, he always had faith. No matter how bad things are, until you're mathematically eliminated, you've got action. That's how I think now. Until we're mathematically eliminated, I don't care. As long as we have one out left, one man left, one breath of air left, we have a chance."

Accountability

Accountability incorporates discipline, faith, and trust. It takes discipline to do the things necessary to be successful. It takes faith to believe that by doing those things goals will be reached. And it takes trust in the expectation that each teammate is doing the same thing. To reach the end goal, players must have faith in the program, the coaching staff, themselves, and their teammates. Moreover, every person has a role on the team, and he must be prepared to fulfill it when called upon to do so.

A large part of each team role is the same for everyone: commitment to the team, commitment to continual self-improvement on and off the field, commitment to helping others, commitment to academic excellence for student-athletes, commitment to integrity, and commitment to family.

Jerry Kindall emphasizes accountability in his team policy: "We have a philosophy that goes beyond the field. We call it 'team policy.' We hold our players at Arizona to a higher standard than most, of personal conduct, personal appearance, personal accountability."

Holding players accountable for their actions is part of instilling discipline. Players not only need discipline, they want it. They may not say it, but they know it makes them better players, better people, and a better team. With personal accountability, players have pride in themselves and the team.

Pride

Having pride is an integral part of the covenant—pride that propels people to do their best, to put in the effort, to reach their potential. It's not the boastful pride or self-promoting actions of an individual with low self-esteem, but the kind of pride that is more unspoken than spoken. It's confidence that comes from having a clear purpose, knowing your goals, and promoting your values, along with teammates who are in the same boat.

Jerry Kindall wanted his teams to have pride on and off the field: "Taking pride on the field is one thing, but we create a better chance to succeed on the field if we're also proud of one another off the field. Whenever we traveled and appeared as a group, we were in coat and tie.

"When I played against the Yankees in 1962, they would come off the bus at the ballpark in coat and tie. They would walk together, and they were proud to be with one another. The Mickey Mantles, the Yogi Berras, the Whitey Fords, the Bobby Richards, they just had an air about them, a presence that was kind of intimidating. They defended one another. They were a presence in the American League. I've never forgotten their great example of team pride."

Kindall saw the results of the Yankees' own covenant. Whether their covenant was in written form or not, they had a distinct way about them—they knew who they were, what they could do, and where they were headed. They were all in it together.

Principle # 2
Form a Covenant

Whether the covenant is written or unwritten, having one is something most championship coaches implement. The key is to have clear goals and a clear value system, starting from the basics of the coach's deepest values, to things he believes will help his players be the best they can be, on and off the field.

This often starts with a mission statement such as LSU's "Excellence both on and off the field." The mission statement is like the thesis, and the covenant is like a longer version outlining the basic mode of operation for the team. The covenant is much more than the team rules: it's a document that says, "This is who we are, and this is how we do things."

The covenant may have a spiritual foundation. The spiritual foundation links the mind, body, and soul to achieve optimal performance. This allows the team to achieve inner focus, concentration, and a warrior spirit.

A good covenant helps create the most synergistic team possible where everyone is working together, pushing each other, supporting each other, and inspiring each other. This is enhanced with teams that have integrity, who take pride in their actions, and trust and respect themselves, their teammates, and the game. When players are accountable to the terms of the covenant, and they are true to themselves and their teammates, then they can reach heights they've never seen before.

CHAPTER 3

Vividly Imagine the End Result

"Anything you vividly imagine, ardently desire, sincerely believe you're worthy of, and enthusiastically act on every day, must come to pass."

— Skip Bertman
Five-time NCAA Division I national champion,
Louisiana State University

At 211 degrees Fahrenheit, water is extremely hot, on the verge of boiling but not quite there. Increase the temperature by one degree and the water becomes alive with activity. That last degree puts it over the top. The chemistry at that temperature causes a strong reaction. At 211 degrees, it is simply hot water, but at 212 degrees, everything changes.

Visualization could be that one degree—the unseen power that changes hope to reality, which puts everything together. Such a small difference exists between winning it all and coming so very close, often inches, but that small margin can make all the difference in the world. Visualization could be that difference.

Just as there is no winning without faith, there is no faith without being able to visualize it first. Superstars grow up imagining being the hero, and it comes to pass. They continually dream and visualize the greatness they've imagined since childhood, and this picture in their mind enables their body to make it happen.

Researchers Find the Imagination Very Powerful

Researchers have found that vividly imagining a skill activates the same areas of the brain as when actually performing the skill—with the exception of the motor cortex, which directs the muscles to produce the movement.[1] If a player vividly imagines getting the game-winning hit, his mind may not be able to tell the difference. If he gets that championship-clinching hit day after day in his mind, when it comes time for the real thing, it will seem like old times.

A person who continually visualizes exactly what he wants and believes he can achieve it, will draw those skills, people, and things he needs to get it done. The universe conspires to make it happen. Those athletes who would be great, and those who are consistently winning, dream big dreams and have grand visions. They imagine their biggest success, then work hard every day toward that vision.

Visualizing the "Impossible" Makes it Possible

One of the biggest challenges for any coach is winning a team's first championship. Without the experience of having done it before, there's often doubt and hesitancy. It's a huge challenge trying to visualize a championship for a team that has never won one. But visualizing is where it starts—it's where all great accomplishments start.

For instance, when the Northwestern University football team upset Notre Dame in 1995, it shocked everyone but themselves—they saw the end result so many times before it actually happened that they expected it to happen, as head coach Gary Barnett explained after the game.

As the game got closer to the end, everyone expected Northwestern to fold. An academic school with a perennial losing record could never beat a national powerhouse, or so most people thought. They didn't fold. In fact, they won. Northwestern had visualized the fourth quarter, and they were prepared for the doubts that would come in the last period. Without visualizing it beforehand, they couldn't have done it, Barnett explained.

In baseball the "impossible" may mean getting the game-winning hit for the championship off the best pitcher in the league. Players have to see it happen first, from the beginning of spring training right up to the actual at-bat. Then, when the actual situation occurs, it will have happened so many times already, he'll be confident and prepared. The impossible becomes possible.

Rod Dedeaux, 11-time NCAA Division I champion at the University of Southern California, saw his team winning it all every year: "We always felt that on opening day, we had the best team in the country. Now, all we had to do was make ourselves that way."

It Starts Early

The first step toward winning a championship, visualizing it happening, begins in childhood. Superstars tell of how when they were young they saw themselves hitting the game-winning home run, or shooting the game-winning basket. They played for hours, often alone, being the hero—every session they went home as the MVP. Today's heroes went home as heroes every day as kids (in their own minds). Dusty Baker did.

"As a kid, we all played those hero games. It was always Baker at the plate, two outs, facing Koufax or Marichal. Or it was always Baker at the free-throw line or Baker with the long touchdown or something. So, you play these games in your mind and it is always you, if you miss you were fouled and had to go to the free throw line or whatever. You made up games so you made sure you won. Then when you get up here (the major leagues), you pretend to be playing the same kinds of games as you did when you were a kid, because you played this game in your mind, over and over a thousand times," Baker explains.

Superstars dreamed about being the hero every day as youngsters, and their dream became reality in adulthood. The dream becomes engrained in their psyche and enables the subconscious to draw it toward them. How many times did Dusty Baker see himself playing in the big leagues before he got there? Every day for twenty years? That's visualization.

He visualized the same ending every time: Baker, the hero. Baker, the star. Baker, the MVP. Every day, day after day. It came to be. Phil Garner did the same thing: "A certain form of visualization is having a dream. [i.e.,] I'm going to be in the World Series. As a kid in high school, I sat and visualized it. I dreamed it. I think visualization is a very, very good technique for players."

In the epic 2001 World Series, the Arizona Diamondbacks pulled out a stunning victory over the powerful Yankees. Luis Gonzalez had the game-winning hit in the bottom of the ninth in game seven. He summed it up: "It's a dream come true. As a little kid you dream about driving in the winning run in the seventh game of the World Series."

Co-MVP Curt Schilling agreed: "Everybody that's ever played the sport has had a wiffle ball in their hand and said, 'It's the seventh game of the World Series and I'm hitting, or pitching.'" Gonzalez and Schilling both dreamed about it when they were young. Repeatedly in their minds they were the heroes in the World Series. Their dreams came true.

Los Angeles Lakers basketball star Kobe Bryant did the same thing. In the 2002 NBA playoffs, he helped put away the San Antonio Spurs with some late-game heroics. When asked about his heroics: "I've dreamed of these situations countless times as a kid, and I still dream of them today," Bryant said.[2]

Dreaming is important because the imagination is so powerful. Hence, fear is such a powerful feeling because it is powered by the imagination. Fear is one of the strongest forces on earth—it prevents people from achieving success more than almost anything else. One thing that is stronger than fear is the power that feeds it, i.e., the imagination. When harnessed, the imagination is the fuel that builds dreams.

Create a Vivid Mental Image

To effectively visualize his dream scenario, a player needs to use all of his senses. A hitter needs to feel the pine tar, smell the popcorn, see the batter's box, and hear the announcer call his name, thereby creating a dramatic mental picture. The pitcher should be able to sense the slope of the mound, feel the stitching on the baseball, smell the leather of his glove, etc.

The visualization process can be enhanced through physically reproducing the act outside of practice, (i.e., going through the hitter's on-deck routine in his room with his bat in his hand). When going through the at-bat, the athlete visualizes a complete sensory environment in a "pressure" situation, and getting the winning base hit. Seeing the actual pitcher and closer (the closer is one of their better pitchers who generally comes in for one inning to "close out" the game) is beneficial. It makes it a more familiar situation to face that pitcher after having seen it in a controlled, successful atmosphere. It will enhance control of emotions.

Rituals can also help facilitate a vivid picture. For example, if a hitter's ritual is to take two deep breaths in the on-deck circle, swing the weighted bat three times, envision himself hitting a line drive the opposite way, and then smile at the crowd, it will soon become automatic. Then, when doing the visualization away from the field, if he continually does the same on-deck routine, with practice, he'll be able to summon some of those same feelings as in the game.

The more often a player can create a vivid picture of a situation, the closer he will be to having actually experienced succeeding in that situation. This is because the subconscious cannot tell the difference between what is vividly imagined and reality. When a player is visualizing, and he actually feels the same feelings he has in the game, then his visualization becomes reality (to his subconscious).

One suggestion for painting a vivid mental picture is to draw up the dream of winning the big game. In other words, have a clear dream for the team and each player. For example, the team dream could be detailing the scene of the championship game (i.e., the competition, the venue, the crowd, the weather, the chaos, the whole scene). Each player can draw up a similar scene with them in the forefront as the hero.

Since the mind works in pictures, getting players to create mental pictures of their own successes is essential. Most athletes remember what they see and hear better than just what they hear. Using as much sensory stimuli as possible to set up a situation may imprint on more players' minds. Gary Adams constantly uses motivational tools such as acting out scenes to help the players remember and utilize the information he's trying to get across. "I'm big on visualization. A picture's worth a thousand words," he says.

"I've done crazy things. I've boxed in front of my players in centerfield. I had the robe on, the headset, the boxing gloves, everything. I wanted to inspire them to keep getting back up. Being a winner doesn't mean not getting knocked down, it means always getting back up. There's crazy things I can't even talk to you about that I've done to motivate my players, inspire them, and teach them. Get their attention! They remember what they see much better, we all do."

Bob Todd believes in using stories to create a picture in his players' minds instead of just telling them what to do. "Many times when I talk to our team, I talk in stories. I try to verbally create situations where players can visualize what I'm talking about. I will never forget the time that this guy was trying to get this AAA pitcher (the highest level of minor league baseball) to throw a strike, and he finally just grabbed the ball and said, 'Here, like this,' and he threw four pitches that were about the nastiest sliders on the black (the outer edges of the plate are referred to as the 'black') and he said, 'That's what I'm talking about!'"

Great coaches enable their players to see themselves performing the skill correctly and succeeding. When the player can see exactly in his mind's eye how to perform the skill, and can also see himself performing the skill well, then he opens up the path to do it well. Todd continues: "What we're really trying to do is verbally communicate effectively to where in that player's mind, he can create a picture for himself."

Once players have a clear vision of success, they need to think about that successful picture daily. Having posters on the wall is an excellent method of affirming the greatness and the success that's forthcoming. Get as many pictures, words, thoughts, and actions focused on the dream as possible.

In 1992, Andy Lopez led the smallest school in NCAA Division I history to the national title. He did this in part by giving the team a clear vision of what it takes to win it all. Every day he would have it clear in his mind and try to clarify it with his players. He explains: "If practice is going magnificently, I will stop and say, 'Hey fellas, *this* is what it takes to get to Omaha.' This type of intensity, this type of efficiency is what gets you to Omaha. So, I give them a vision. So they know, 'Oh, this is what he wants'. And since I've been there, I have some credibility, and they say, 'Aw, so you mean if we do it this way all the time, we'll get there.' On the other side of the coin, if I see a horrible practice, I'll stop it and say, 'Guys, you've got no shot to ever see it unless you fly over it, the way that you're working. With this type of intensity, this type of efficiency, forget it. You guys will never experience it.' So we give them a vision both ways. I don't see myself as a motivator; I see myself as a visionary. I will give you that vision, and we will live that vision. We're going to work like crazy to bring that vision to fruition."

Videos Can Trigger Proper Mental State

A big way to enhance visualization is to put the dream into still pictures, videos, and/or written messages. Playing videos of previous successes or championship games in the clubhouse can be hugely beneficial. Skip Bertman has used this technique to the tune of five NCAA Division I national championships in 10 years.[3] His clubhouse is full of pictures and tangible images of success. They watch a video of their past successes before *every* game.[4]

This ritual not only motivates his players in pregame, but also jumpstarts the mental zone he wants his players to be in. The video shows the players in the "zone," that ideal performance state that allows peak performance. It shows their excitement, the crowd, the intensity, and, importantly, the players succeeding amidst all the chaos.

Highlight videos can inspire players when they are feeling down, prompt players when they need to practice harder, or motivate players in the off-season when the first game is four months away. They take players back to that great play, that awesome game, those feelings, and the memory of what they did and how they did it. Ron Polk relies heavily on videotape: "We videotape a lot: hitters, pitchers, infielders, outfielders. We think it's very, very important. It's an aspect of our program we really feel is vital. They see themselves on tape every day, batting practice included."

Videos allow players to use their memory, and not let their memory use them. Every athlete who has played for any length of time has great memories and poor ones, and he chooses what to do with each. If he focuses on the bad ones, his self image may suffer.

Andy Lopez says that visualization is the foundation of his program. "I'm a visionary. I give guys the vision of success, the vision of excellence. If you come to my program, I'm going to give you a vision of playing in Omaha (the College World Series venue in Nebraska). That's my vision. Every day we talk about Omaha. The NCAA sends out a video to every Division I coach of the prior year's World Series. We played that video every day at Pepperdine in the clubhouse. They had to watch Omaha every day. They got sick of it, until they actually got there, and they became the highlight. We talk about it every single day.

See the Positives

A large part of visualization is being able to eliminate the negative thoughts and replace them with thoughts of success. So much negativity exists in such a failure-filled game that it's hard to keep it in check sometimes. The great players have programmed their minds to persevere and make it happen. Rod Delmonico, head coach at Tennessee, explains: "You have to see yourself having success. The problem with kids, or anybody, is that they play it back negatively. I *can't* do this, I *can't* do that, and they visualize it over and over in their head. What I encourage them to do is to visualize it in their mind, change the picture to you *can* win, you *can* be the guy that hits it out of the ballpark, you *can* be the guy that comes in and strikes the guy out, or you can be the guy that makes the great play after you've made a bad play. You've got to change the picture.

"Great players do it naturally. They have such an unbelievable belief system, that they can go out there and look bad one night, and realize that it was just that the odds got them. And they can bounce back the next day and be the hero. You have to credit mom and dad and their family upbringing that did something to teach them how to be a winner. That's what we try to do," Delmonico says.

The best athletes are able to forget the bad plays and remember the good ones. They seem to have their own mental videos they replay over and over. Videos can accentuate the good memories and imprint them in the mind so even average athletes can also have great mental videos.

Imprinting the memories of past successes is crucial to future success. In fact, it may not be possible to win a championship without it. Dusty Baker talks about the importance of having a selective memory: "If you get beat 14-3, you have to turn around and forget yesterday's game. But if you win 2-1 and you had a great play to win the game, or you had a game-winning single or home run or whatever, I want you to remember it, and remember the feeling that you had prior to going up there to the plate or making that play."

Tom Trebelhorn uses videos to facilitate the proper mental state and to take the successes of the past and make those memories a part of the future: "I might take all the catcher's great throws, tags at the plate, diving plays of a pop-up, double-play pivots, blocking the plate, all the really good stuff, and just show the catchers. Look how great you are! Or the hitters—all the good swings. Or the outfielders—all the great plays."

"We keep highlight tapes that every once in a while, when I think that particular area might be feeling kind of bad about themselves, I bring them in. For instance, hitters—look at how we can hit, boom, boom, boom. Because they're very visual learners. I think tapes work and they love to see themselves do well; that image helps them forget the image that might not be working out too good right now. I really like positive highlight tapes. They come to the park the day after a loss and I'll have a tape on of an outfielder's great catch, and you'll start talking about baseball again, good stuff," Trebelhorn continues.

When teams are losing, everything seems to drop a notch. Players begin to argue and they start talking about things unrelated to baseball, and the team chemistry can take a beating. Videos can help stimulate that good chemistry.

Trebelhorn uses videos in pregame or whenever necessary: "After a tough game I might say, 'Come here guys, look at this, isn't this great?' Maybe we were really lousy. It makes me feel better to watch that stuff too. Because it's easy to go into a shell and say, 'oh poor me, poor us.' Pretty soon you're not looking forward to the next day. Stop it right there and focus on something positive and get ready for the next day because, chances are, it's going to be better. Might as well get ready."

Imprinting success on the player's mind comes from visualization, good memories, and seeing it over and over. Terry Collins creates an atmosphere that allows that to happen: "We tape every game. In our video room we can show a player's bad at-bat next to a good at-bat. At the end of the year, our players are given a tape of only their good at-bats. That's one kind of visualization we do.

"For our pitchers, we put together some of their best innings. So, when they're watching that, they see what they're doing. I don't want them to see their mistakes; they're going to have mistakes. What I want them to do is look at what they've been doing properly so the more they see that and the more they continue to try and stay in that frame, I think it breaks slumps faster, using videos. I think players get out of slumps a lot quicker than they used to because of the fact that they can see what they're physically doing wrong," Collins states.

Video taping is a technology that is such a huge bonus for players of this generation that former players didn't have. Not only do videos enable players to compare good technique and form versus poor form, but, they also seal the picture in the player's minds.

Trebelhorn elaborates: "I think tapes are the best visualization technique there is. Because that is an external image that shows them success after success after success. And also, baseball is a very individualistic game. When you're showing highlights of several players, whether it be outfielders, infielders, catchers, pitchers, hitters—they're seeing others too on their team doing well. I found the tapes to really be the best visualization technique."

Imprint the Night Before

A great time to visualize is the night before the game. Players should see the next day's pitcher or hitters, and see themselves in possible scenarios coming through in the clutch. Experts agree that lots of small visualization sessions are better than one long session (the power of repetition). Similarly, visualizing the night before is better than getting up early and doing it the same day (although both is ideal). Going through an at-bat or pitching to a batter for five to ten minutes every night before a game is all that needs to be done—it doesn't have to be long.

Phil Garner likes his players to visualize at night: "I tell players I used visualization right before I went to sleep at night. I'd visualize individual performance, game performance, and then I'd visualize a situation. Bases loaded, game's on the line in the World Series, and, wouldn't you know, the situation came up. Wouldn't you know that I did just what I visualized I was going to do? It was 20 years later, but it happened. So, you get players to focus on the fact that if you do these things, they will come true."

Carroll Land uses visualization the night before and as part of every pregame: "We talk about a commitment to at least a 30-minute visualization the night before we play. We see ourselves doing things at the very best level, things we love to do. We do it again just before the game starts, in groups. The hitters are all with the offensive coach, and the pitchers are with my assistant pitching coach. They're all sitting there visualizing, while I am dealing with the ground rules getting the game started. It's a five-minute visualization, a quiet time in groups with somebody leading them through the visualization."

Rod Delmonico does the same thing at Tennessee: "I tell our guys to dream. I encourage them, when they go to bed at night, to think about winning a national championship. To think about being the guy that hits the home run, that makes the diving play, that backhands the ball and throws it across the infield, or that gets a base hit with the bases loaded."

Imprinting the vision the night before is often done with a bat in hand. Here's how a hitter might go about it: before bed, the hitter grabs his bat and takes his stance. Then, he goes through an entire at-bat facing the toughest pitcher in the league, making sure it's a pressure situation and the odds are stacked against him. Maybe the pitcher's throwing a one-hitter and it's a 1-0 game with two outs in the ninth, and a runner on second. He gets two quick strikes with the nastiest sliders on the black the hitter's ever seen. What's he to do? Most people would give up mentally, but not him. He visualizes fouling a few off, takes a couple of close pitches, then lines the next pitch into the right-center gap to tie the game.

If players can vividly imagine getting the game-winning hit, their minds will get used to the "pressure", and they start to crave the excitement, and chaos. Getting that championship-clinching hit night after night during visualization allows the real thing to flow smoothly. The hitter will have done it so many times, his mind and body will be prepared for it. He'll be able to focus on the at-bat and enjoy the competition.

Visualize Pressure Situations in the Upcoming Series

The night before the first game of a series, teams can start visualizing for that series. Hitters visualize the next day's starting pitcher and the relievers they expect to face. They'll visualize what they look like, what their tendencies are, and their attitude. Is the pitcher an intense competitor? If so, then look for him to have an ego about his best pitch—whether it's throwing the ball past hitters, or making hitters miss their slider.

For example, if a guy throws 95 mph, chances are he doesn't have much of a change-up, or anything else. If he did, he'd be in the big leagues! So, that's great. He throws 95 mph. Get in the back of the box, spit on (meaning don't swing at) anything but the fastball, and get ready just a bit earlier. See the pressure situations against the next opponent, and visualize the coming success.

In professional baseball or on a college road trip, teams play each other three or four times in a row. For example, maybe the Durham Bulls are traveling to play the Winston-Salem Spirits. To enhance their visualization, the Bulls could take out their highlight film against the Spirits (ideally the team has a highlight video of themselves against every team in the league). They should watch all the great plays ever made against their opponents, and any big wins against them. Visualizing success is important and extremely beneficial. Visualizing success in pressure situations against the upcoming opponent with the use of videos, photos, and any other implement makes visualization extremely efficient.

Some teams utilize visualization as part of their pregame. Successful players do it in their own way before every game, and some championship teams do it together in pregame. Jerry Kindall's championship teams used visualization before road trips: "We've done that [visualize], with hitters especially. And pitchers fine-tuning. Jerry [Stitt, Kindall's assistant, before becoming head coach] has an exercise where they lie down on the field and close their eyes and he helps them visualize what's going to happen as we go on this road trip. He's really done very well at that."

Visualize the Moment Before the Big Moment

One of the often overlooked but very important aspects of visualizing is seeing the moments right before and right after the big moment. It is fairly obvious that seeing success in the toughest situation is imperative. All big performers have felt that feeling right before the "pressure" situation. Either they are totally focused and in the moment, or they are out of sync. When focused, players have a confidence and maybe cockiness that contributes to their success.

A feeling of knowing they're going to succeed, an inner peace, a confidence and determination exists that players should visualize. Seeing the moments surrounding the big moment is important as well. They should see themselves on the bus or plane feeling the confidence. If they're riding the bus for two hours to go to the biggest game of their life, they should see themselves relaxed and ready on the bus, preparing with confidence, everything flowing smoothly. Next, they should see themselves in the moment before the moment, then the moment, and then the moment after.

Play the Game Before the Game:
See Every Possible Scenario

Visualization not only encompasses seeing the crucial moments, but also seeing every possible scenario. It means a player continually sees himself being successful in any situation that may come up. If he's seen it before, he'll be prepared and able to react instinctively when it happens, rather than having to first react cognitively.

Being mentally prepared means never being surprised by anything. In the article *The Mental Edge*, William F. Allman states that Hall of Fame quarterback Fran Tarkenton would visualize every possible situation that might arise during play. Tarkenton not only wanted to be ready for every play, but he also wanted to be able to react instinctively and successfully.[5]

Mike Hargrove explains what he does: "I try to imagine worst-case scenarios, and how I will react and take care of those situations, both as a player when I played and as a manager now. And that prepares you for whatever comes along."

US Olympic gold medallist skier Picabo Street saw herself going down the run over and over in her mind before her event. She saw every turn, every bump, every obstacle and visualized flying by in perfect harmony.[6] She won her gold medal by 1/100 of a second. The great athletes see themselves succeeding before it actually happens, and they see themselves succeeding in a vast number of possible scenarios.

Having seen all the scenarios and having experienced them over and over is what makes visualization such a powerful tool. This preparation brings confidence to the visualization, which is a big help in drawing upon more sights, sounds, and senses to paint the picture.

Imprinting different scenarios in players' minds allows them to react intensely, automatically, and fluidly when the situation occurs on the field. For example, imagine playing right field and there's a wall that juts out by the bullpen (i.e., War Memorial Stadium in Greensboro, NC). Being mentally prepared means watching balls hit down the line in batting practice and seeing how they bounce off that wall, fielding them, and visualizing throwing the runner out at second. It also means reviewing possible scenarios such as the one just described between pitches during the game.

Here's a typical scenario: an outfielder carefully watches the opponent's base runners and identifies who likes to run, watching the top and bottom of the order very closely. He's watching to see if one of those guys will try to take an extra base on him, or if someone has an ego that says if he hits a ball down the line, he will go two no matter what. The outfielder visualizes the ball hit down the line, he hustles over there, spins, and throws the guy out at second base. If he knows ahead of time that he is going two on a ball down the line, then he's going to bust his behind to get there and make a great play when it happens. Great plays happen because players see it happen first. Then great innings happen, and then great games. Consequently, championships are won.

Tom Trebelhorn visualizes possible scenarios for his team that invariably come to pass. Especially in big games, Trebelhorn will motivate the team by predicting situations and having players see themselves succeeding in these possible scenarios. He is able to do this by knowing the other team, remembering past games, and knowing his team.

Trebelhorn describes what he does: "I've had fairly good success in setting up scenarios that come true. [For example,] you're going to go out and lead this game off and we're going to do this, this, and this. They kind of focus on that, and then it might happen. I try to have them focused on this is how the outcome's going to be, and be ready to do this, this, and this.

"I've had a reasonable amount of luck picking out things that work for that particular club on that particular day. I think once they have an image of success or something positive, it helps take some of the pressure off that's created on a big game. If they take that and focus on this very narrow thing, generally it might not come perfectly true but you're moving toward this kind of a game plan."

Going through all possible scenarios is tantamount to proper preparation. Tom House explains: "Play the game before the game. You sit down with your catcher and your defense, and you pre-pitch every hitter. Try to create as many situations as you can, based on what you've seen on video and scouting reports. If you've played the game before the game, now when the game is happening, you've already been there. Then, it's just basically connecting the dots during the game. I think that's probably been the biggest lesson I've learned in the last 10 years."

Playing the game before the game involves many things but mostly, it's putting players in a position where they've seen any situation that might arise in an actual game, on video, and/or in their mind. This allows things to flow smoothly during the game, as if the players knew what was coming.

Generally, baseball follows a predictable story line. The starting pitcher usually goes five or six innings, then a reliever is brought in for an inning or two. In the eighth or ninth the closer is brought in. It's especially predictable for better hitters, as they will always try to match their best pitchers against your best hitters.

If the cleanup hitter is up in a close game in the sixth inning with runners on base, and their starter has gone the distance, be ready for them to bring their best middle reliever. If it's later in the game, look for their closer. On top of that, look for his best pitch—at least be ready for it. Closers generally have a mentality that allows for predictability. Often, they'll have one pitch that they rely heavily on. For closers, it's usually a good fastball or a hard slider. So, against the clean-up hitter, with the bases loaded and a full count, what's he going to throw? Obviously, his best pitch. Visualize it and look for it when the situation arises. But more importantly, look for it the night before during visualization.

Pitchers can do the same thing with hitters. Many hitters are so concerned with not being behind the fastball (i.e., swinging too late) that they are often out in front on slower pitches. Pitchers can use this to their advantage and visualize this in the game.

When a pitcher is able to vividly envision intricate details of his best performance, then his game can flow fairly harmoniously. Different scenarios get handled with instinctive reactions instead of surprised reactions, and bang-bang plays may get called more in the pitcher's favor.

Playing the game before the game as a hitter means knowing who the umpire will be, what his strike zone is generally like, who the pitcher and catcher will be, etc. It's knowing every pitch a pitcher has, what he is throwing for strikes that day, who is likely to come in to relieve and how he will pitch, what the umpire's zone is that day, etc. This is pictured in the hitter's mind the night before the game, the day of the game, and during pregame. This type of pre-playing the game helps instincts take over rather than reactions.

Linking the Mind and Body

When a player's instincts take over—when they can react immediately without thought or concern—then they can make the great play that would otherwise have been the short end of the stick. In a game where inches and split-seconds count, this is crucial.

Getting the mind to work in concert with the body is the goal of every great athlete, and baseball is no exception. The martial arts are excellent at achieving this: Zen, for example, sets this as a goal. Sixteenth century samurai Miyamoto Musashi describes the Japanese practice of Zen as an awareness, a heightened sense of feeling and sensitivity that one develops in doing what comes naturally.[7] He talks about athletes who move so fluidly and gracefully, they seem effortless. Their mental and physical practice allows such fluidity.

Musashi elaborates: "If you want to see, see right at once. When you begin to think, you miss the point...the idea is, of course, not to intellectualize the experience." With Zen the mind is clear and focused solely on the moment, and each moment that comes there seems to be no physical or cognitive "reaction," only prepared "preaction."

When Picabo Street hits those bumps, she doesn't react. Picabo "preacts." Not only did she know when the bump was going to be around the next corner, but she also knew how she was going to use that bump physically to propel her around the turn. Cognitively, she didn't have to think about it, it was as fluid as if she knew it was coming. She did.

Hitters can do the same thing by seeing the pitcher, knowing the pitcher, knowing situations, and "preacting," not reacting. When that hard-throwing righty brushes the hitter off the plate with a 93 mph fastball on an 0-2 count, then comes back with a slider away, the hitter can "preact." The hitter has prepared, which means he doesn't have to think. He can just stay confident in the moment and wait for the pitch to come to him, then drive the ball to the opposite field, almost as if he was looking for it. He is able to hit the ball where it is pitched in a difficult situation because his reaction is instinctive.

The great hitters have visualized scenarios so they can respond as if they knew what was coming. It's so fluid, like Zen. Mike Hargrove used visualization which enhanced his "preaction:" "Anytime you can visualize what it is you need to do in certain situations, when those situations arise, there's not a whole lot of thought that has to go into it. You can react in the proper sequence and the proper way to those situations," he explains.

Visualize During the Game

An important adjunct to visualizing before competition is doing so during an actual game. For example, the on-deck circle is an important visualizing place. Each hitter can see himself hitting the ball in the gap, or over the second baseman's head, or up the middle. And like the great players, they learn from their mistakes and focus on the good plays—seeing them over and over and remembering the feeling.

During the 2002 World Series, the Anaheim Angels had some unlikely heroes come through in the clutch. When Anaheim was on the verge of elimination during Game 6, Scott Spiezio hit a three-run home run to ignite the rally that brought the momentum and the series to Anaheim. How did this happen?

It started many years ago, in Spiezio's childhood. The *San Francisco Chronicle* reported that Spiezio, "has been through Game 7 many times before—usually in his back yard."[8] Spiezio's father Ed, who won World Series rings with the St. Louis Cardinals in 1964 and 1967, taught him the value of visualization. Television cameras caught Spiezio sitting motionless in the dugout with his eyes closed after his seventh inning home run. He said, "I was just going over the feeling again, trying to remember it. It's helpful after successful at-bats to try and embed it into your head. At the same time, it also helps you focus in on your next at-bat, too."

Spiezio grew up imagining the dramatic home run in his back yard, then he visualized it happening, then it happened, then he visualized it after it happened. How did a wild card team picked to finish last in their division win a World Series? Just ask Spiezio how he did it.

Principle #3
Vividly Imagine the End Result

Visualization is one of the most powerful tools in athletics and in any major accomplishment. What a man consistently thinks about, he moves towards. If he sows thoughts of a championship-clinching hit or pitch, night after night, his subconscious (which cannot tell the difference between reality and that which is vividly imagined), will attract it.

Phil Garner describes it: "What you think, what your heart's desire is what you'll end up with. It's almost like putting your heart and your head in such a mode that says I want it, and somehow it comes to you.

Players become what they think about, believe in, and vividly imagine, and when an environment of success surrounds them, they have the best chance of absorbing it. To be a player who reacts instinctively to any situation, who is aggressive when the pressure's on, and who comes through in the clutch, he needs to be good at seeing it in his mind.

Champions have a crystal clear picture of what winning the championship looks like and feels like. They may have pictures of it on their walls, they may watch videos of it, and most importantly, they vividly imagine it. Champions reach a point where that detailed, dramatic image of themselves and their team being successful is easily pictured in their minds.

CHAPTER 4

Develop Team Chemistry

"Building team chemistry is one of the most important things we try to do. It's probably contributed more to our success than anything."

— Ed Cheff
12-time NAIA national champion,
Lewis-Clark State University

Championship teams have a certain aura about them. It shows in the way they walk, the way they talk, their banter in the clubhouse, and, of course, in the way they perform on the field. They have confidence in themselves, their skills, and their teammates, and that synergy unifies them. The players may or may not be great friends, but they respect each other and work together in a way that makes the sum total of their respective selves much greater than they would be as 25 individuals.

Championship coaches develop that synergy by building the players' confidence and communicating the ideals of the covenant, which keeps them focused and pulls them together as a team. They also allow their players the freedom to create some energy within the team, while maintaining the discipline to do the things that help them win. Championship coaches develop teammates who trust and respect each other and put the team first—then they have chemistry.

Energy in the Clubhouse

Championship-type athletes have a fire burning within them that promotes them to continually seek out competition. When they play, they want to win, and it generally doesn't matter what they're playing. They may be professional baseball players, but if they're playing ping-pong, they're going to give it everything they've got. It's like bears hunting salmon, they're serious about the task. It's almost instinctive—competition brings out this aggressive nature.

These athletes also have confidence, heaps of it. That confidence may turn into cockiness, but this enables them to do what they do. Without it, they might not have the same edge. Phil Garner, major league baseball player and manager, has seen this with the championship teams he's been on. They've got a little bit of an attitude. "Good teams always have an arrogance about them. They're confident they know what to do. They know they know what to do; therefore, they do it. You're not going to surprise them in tough situations," he says.

Winning managers are able to take this arrogance, this intensity, and harness it. They use it to propel the team to reach it's potential. It's like when a fire is out of control, it can be damaging, but when used effectively, it can be a torch that burns very bright.

When harnessed, the "arrogance" becomes an energy that can motivate teammates to succeed on the field rather than becoming a damaging force. The "arrogant" energy is turned into competitive energy, which also helps compel their teammates to get a little of that same fire in them. Phil Garner explains: "One ingredient from all the winning teams I've seen is that players push each other, police each other. A manager is part of it, but great managers without personnel can't win. So the manager is only as good as the personnel. And the personnel are only as good as the fire that burns in them.

"Every good team that I've been on, which includes the Oakland A's, the Cincinnati Reds, and Pittsburgh Pirates, had those ingredients. The players control a lot, not everything, but a lot. And they set the tone. You've got to have energy in the clubhouse, all the good teams have it."

Garner continues: "Probably the most important ingredient is you have to have individual players that are willing and have the guts to speak up and say, 'Shoot, you guys aren't catching the ball very good are you, you guys aren't hitting it very good are you, you guys aren't pitching it very good are you?' You've got to have some sort of that banter.

"That breeds competition among the different segments within the team: competition among pitchers, between pitchers and hitters, among infielders, between a guy that's hitting third and a guy that's hitting fifth…anytime you get this interplay that one wants to do better than the other, as long as it doesn't get out of hand. There's got to be some one-upmanship there; there has to be a certain banter that's put about in the clubhouse."

It's been said that iron sharpens iron, and with some energy in the clubhouse, sparks may begin to fly. When talented players are assembled, there may be some friction. There may even be physical confrontations, but it's how that affects their play on the field that's most important. Sometimes star players push and motivate each other through competition or even conflict. At other times, those same players may end up in a physical conflict. Thomas Jefferson said, "I feel that a little rebellion now and then is a good thing." Jefferson realized that in this context, that those top people do have an internal fire. They may have a different, or even better, way of doing things. A little rebellion, some energy that gets people worked up, a fire that's not always copasetic with the status quo, those may not be bad things.

Garner continues: "To create a certain atmosphere, I try to stimulate it a little bit. I might not call them on the carpet if there's a fight. I try to encourage a little bit of that. Because when you're stuck with these guys for 180 days out of the year, if you've got some fire in your belly, you're going to take exception to some things sometimes; you're going to fight. You're going to want to fight, that's the way it is. So you want to create that atmosphere where there's some honesty, some competition, and some pride. When you do all that, and throw all that together, sometimes it's going to boil a little bit, but I think that's good."

The last team to win three World Series' in a row, the 1972 – 1974 Oakland A's had some friction, some confrontations. But the chemistry they had did the job on the field. They did those things Garner mentioned: they competed, they had pride, they were honest, and they didn't hide their conflicts.

Pitching coach and psychologist Tom House explains this odd chemistry: "Successful teams have a sense of camaraderie, even if they fight off the field. [They have] a covenant, if you will, on the field. The Oakland A's were a perfect example of that. They fought like cats and dogs in the clubhouse and off the field, but when they went between the lines, they put it together. Billy North and Reggie Jackson may have had a fist fight at three o'clock in the afternoon, but if somebody knocked Reggie down, then the whole team—Billy North included—fought for that occurring to Reggie."

Garner explains why this is OK: "You don't always have to be hunky dory, peachy keen. You're going to lock horns sometimes. Players create that energy. There's always an ebb and flow with a good ball club. Sometimes it gets out of hand, and the great clubs I've been on, it's never been too low. It's always been a high-energy kind of scenario. They can't do the part of it that I should do, but I can't do the part of it that they should do. No manager can. You need players that are high energy."

Ed Cheff has had a lot of talented players go through his system, including over 80 that went on to play professionally. They didn't always get along, but they won in spite of that. The talent and energy that those top players had sometimes spawned clashes with each other, but they had enough respect for the team to put their differences aside on the field.

Cheff explains one situation he encountered: "One time at the national championship we had two guys get in a fight at breakfast the day of the championship game. They both left—I just broke them up. I'm going, this is driving me crazy, and yet that night they played catch together in the pregame. They never really did like each other, but I think they figured out, just to show the rest of the players that we're still together when we're on the field, they played catch together. I noticed that and thought that was interesting...but they never were close, so there were never any pretenses."

Great players have an aura and energy that radiates. When this energy rubs off onto teammates and they begin to compete with and motivate each other, it can create an electric atmosphere.

Get One Player to Step Forward

Championship teams have this energy because they have leaders who step forward, lead by example, and watch the others to make sure they follow in line. They don't expect the manager to do all the leading; he couldn't even if he wanted to. He has to delegate responsibility, and allow some freedom of expression within the confines of the team.

Terry Francona explains: "The one thing that jumps out at me right away is having one guy, one very visible guy that can raise his hand on the bus or in the middle of the clubhouse and say, 'Whoa, slow down.' He has the ability, even if it's not loud, to say that, guys like Andre Dawson. Every good team has someone like that."

That one guy stepping forward, at least one guy, draws the players together. It's as if the manager presents the plan, and somebody has to say, "Yes, let's do this. This will work. I believe in the coach's plan and I'm going to do my part. You better too." Without that one guy, many players who aren't too sure what they want, will be wishy-washy. They may not buy into the vision. They may have doubts and not work quite as hard as they could, because nobody stepped forward to confirm the coach's plan.

At least one guy has to provide some leadership because if nobody does, there's going to be little groups of players (cliques), that do their own thing. And they won't have that energy, that fire, at least not the type that pushes and motivates one another. In addition, the energy they do have may be wasted, like a fire burning out of control rather than acting as a united force that radiates energy.

Terry Collins knows the importance of getting a few players to take a leadership role: "There's never been a team where 25 guys liked all 24 other guys on the team. You have to have some leadership in the clubhouse. I don't think the manager or the coaches can do it all. You have to have somebody who's willing to step up and take control of some things; you try to find those guys.

"Every good team has one of those guys that are willing to step forward and say, 'I don't care what you think of me personally, but this is how we're supposed to do it here.' Probably one of the best I was ever around was Ken Caminiti. He plays the game one way."

The ability to lead comes with experience, but it also comes with desire, and prior winning. Guys who have been there, who have reached the pinnacle, realize that it takes a coach with a clear plan and players who buy into it, along with players who encourage others to do the same. "They know what it takes to play, and they're not afraid to say something to the next guy, irregardless of how the guy feels, because they know what it takes to be successful. I think what you end up doing, is drawing more and more guys into that corner, and all of the sudden everyone wants to be in that group. So those leaders in the clubhouse are big," Collins explains.

Putting the Team First

Those leaders in the clubhouse do one very important thing: They put the team first and expect the others to do the same. They work together on the field and play as a team. Every player fills his role when called upon. Some teams can do this with guys who don't get along off the field because they work together on the field.

Even though a player may hate another guy on the team, he would take a pitch if the other player needed to steal, he would bunt him over if the situation called for it, or he would make contact on a hit-and-run. The two players who dislike each other know it's not about them. It's about all 25 guys on the team. Players may not see eye to eye, but if they are mature enough and respectful enough to take care of their responsibilities, they can win despite their differences. This is because they have a certain measure of respect for the team, and with the covenant, they can see how they can win.

They know that for the individual to be the greatest he can be, the team must also be great. MVP awards are not typically given to players on last place teams.[1] When players can put aside individual differences for the good of the team, each player's game (i.e., level of play) gets raised. Players must recognize that they all need each other. There is no individual success without team success.

If one guy steps forward, it snowballs. The coach puts out the plan, one guy not only believes in it, but he also follows it and pushes others to it. Then the guys who were on the fringe, the one's who weren't really certain if the plan could work or if the team had enough talent to win, start joining in. They put aside personal differences knowing that it's the only way they can all achieve success.

When players put the team first, it helps everyone. And everyone is important on a championship team. Ken Knutson, head coach at the University of Washington, describes the importance of chemistry in the team: "There are 37 guys on our team, and everybody is really important. If you want to be the number one draft pick, an All-

American, or the winner of a national championship, you need those guys to help you, right? If you are an awesome hitter and the guy behind you can't hit, you will not get anything to hit, you will not be an All-American. You need that guy. You all need each other. So I put it on them."

Putting the team first doesn't mean putting the individual second. Putting the team first elevates the individual. If a player does what is necessary to help his teammates, they will not only help him in return, but they will also be stronger as a team. Presenting a unified front allows the individual player more room to be successful. Tom House tells his teams: "You can pick your friends when the season is over, right now you have to figure out a way that you guys can win as a group, because you can be successful as an individual, but you only win as a group."

When a player constantly puts himself first, he often isolates himself. His teammates won't be as likely to assist him or help elevate his play, and it becomes a struggle for everyone to maintain their focus. Kevin Towers discusses egos: "I think team chemistry is huge. One reason why our club has been successful the last couple of years is because there are no egos. I think you've got to leave your ego aside; there's always somebody that can replace you."

Winning a championship takes teamwork. Whether that means getting along off the field or not depends on the team. Some teams are able to overcome problems off the field or personality clashes and still win. They may win despite their clashes, but they may win partially because of their energy, which leads to clashes.

"The 1979 Pittsburgh Pirates 'We are Family', was BS. I mean we had common goals, but we had guys from well-to-do white neighborhoods, we had guys from the ghettos, and we had guys from Latin American countries who didn't grow up with blankets on their beds," Garner explains.

Teams with good chemistry put it all together on the field and do what it takes to win. It can be supported by the players developing tolerance, trust, and integrity amongst themselves. Terry Francona describes it: "I think to be a winner you have to have dedicated players that put the ball club first. When you have a group of players, regardless of how they get along, who are willing to put the ball club first, you always have a chance to win."

Ed Cheff, winner of 12 national championships at Lewis-Clark State University, talks about it: "One of the key things in winning is the makeup between different types of guys. The A's didn't even pretend to like each other, yet when they went out on the field they flat out won. Some teams, you need that team chemistry to win; I've had teams that hated each other that won."

Somehow some of Cheff's teams and the A's of the early 70's won despite their lack of camaraderie. They won because they didn't take their personal likes and dislikes between the lines. They had the pride, determination, and maturity to know that they needed each other on the field for anyone to have success.

Be Clear About Responsibilities

Whether players on the team are a close-knit group, or they fight off the field, it's important to provide a very detailed, organized structure for the team. Especially if they're not getting along well, they need to have some stability. They need to know what they can count on.

Being organized allows players to know what their role is and how they fit in. They know exactly what they should be doing and when. And they know what to expect from the manager and what he expects from them. This comes in part from having the players sign a covenant at the beginning of the year.

Ed Cheff explains what he does: "We try to give them a formula, a team chemistry formula. I'll give them about an hour to talk about what we want to do as far as team chemistry. Your responsibilities, my responsibilities, and we're responsible together to do this. So, we try to be clear what their responsibilities are, what mine are. Clear communication is important so there's no question. [For example], were we really not supposed to drink on this trip, or what was the curfew, or my social situation, you really don't want me to do that in the community…you know so that things are clear."

A coaching staff that is organized communicates to the players that the team is focused and in the position to be successful. It gives them confidence and freedom to integrate their little quirks within the boundaries of the team. Future Hall-of-Famer Wade Boggs used to have his personal pregame routine timed to the minute (in addition to eating chicken before each game). Everything he did was on a strict schedule. If the team is unorganized, this is impossible. If pregame infield (the defensive warm-up just prior to the game) is supposed to start at 7 p.m., and it starts at 7:05, that will throw some players off, like Boggs.

Being organized means not only sticking to the schedule and being on time, but also the entire coaching staff working together in harmony. If one coach says one thing, and another coach says another, that lack of togetherness can disrupt chemistry. Dusty Baker believes being organized is vital to promoting good chemistry: "Number one, I believe that the coach and staff have to mesh first in order to show the players that we are organized, and that we believe in precision and also communication. I think that communication is huge. In most places people do not communicate enough."

When the coaching staff is organized, it displays excellent non-verbal communication. If everything is completely laid out, and everyone knows their role and where they're supposed to be, then less time is needed to explain things and more time is available to motivate. Players are great to work with when they have a clear plan and are motivated to follow it.

Terry Collins explains: "I think being organized is a huge factor. So is discipline. If you're self-disciplined and organized, players fall in line. People want to be led. I really believe that. So if you show them that, 'hey, I'm willing to be the guy that you can follow,' they'll give you a little extra effort."

Tom Trebelhorn is a great motivator. It could be in part due to his enthusiasm and organization: "I try to lead by example and be very organized so they know what's happening. I think any player that knows what's going to happen or how we're going to handle a situation will be motivated to handle that situation." When players know how they fit in, and what's expected of them, they have a much better chance of contributing.

The 25th Man

When championship teams win, it means everyone has contributed. Everyone from the bat boys to the manager, feels like they have an important role on the team. The great managers make even the bat boy feel his role is as important as anyone else's. They make the last player on the end of the bench, the (twenty-fifth guy), feel like he's just as important as the rest of the players.

This is essential for two important reasons. First, in baseball the outcome of a game may be thrust on the shoulders of the last player on the bench, so he needs to be ready. Second, if he doesn't accept his role, not only will he be unprepared, he'll also distract others from doing their best by his negative attitude. And dissension can be disastrous if not addressed. If one player brings a negative attitude to the field every day, that can spread and disrupt the team.

Often baseball will come down to the least likely hero, or the seldom-used bench player who is suddenly needed in the championship game. That's why there is a need to prepare the twenty-fifth guy; the last guy needs to be ready to go in and execute. A good sign of team chemistry is when your twenty-fifth guy comes off the bench in the ninth to help the team win. He hasn't seen the field in three weeks, yet he comes through. He's been pulling for his guys, and he's always ready.

Davey Johnson, 1997 American League Manager of the Year, explains: "Chemistry is when everything fits. When you have 25 guys that feel a part of something, that are contributing. Even the twenty-fifth guy, that's probably the most important guy. Knowing what he needs to do to be successful, so he's going to be happy, so he's going to be prepared, so he's going to be ready when you call on him. I think one of my strengths is using all twenty-five guys. Giving them the opportunity. After I've chosen the ones that I feel are important to make up this team that have a chance to bond together."

Jim Dietz agrees: "The idea is learning to use your personnel and getting them to buy into these roles and, if you can do that, then you have a chance to be successful. The thing is, nobody likes to sit on the bench so the biggest challenge for a coach in baseball is to get the people to understand that they do have value even though they're not actively in the start of that game because they could be in it at the end when it's the biggest.

"In baseball you can play for three hours and the game can end in a second. You can play and play and play and it can be one pitch, one error, could be anything. That's the way baseball is and you have to get that concept across to your players and they have to buy into it, and if they do, then you have a chance to be successful."

One of the most important ways of getting the twenty-fifth player to accept his role is to look for opportunities to use him in that role. If you use him in that role, whenever it comes up, even if it's only once a month, he'll be ready. Davey Johnson explains: "As a manager you have to make sure you give them the opportunity to fulfill their role on the ball club, so they're feeling they're going to have an opportunity to do something special for the team, no matter how big or small."

Develop Autonomy

In conjunction with giving players some leeway to push and police each other, coaches may try to let the team have its own personality within the confines of the rules and the team vision. Autonomy is letting players do their job and be themselves, which can enhance their motivation.

Tom House tries to give his teams leeway, some autonomy to let their personalities come through: "Basically let the team be the team. You can't mandate who can be friends, but you can mandate against things that will cause chemistry problems. You integrate the ballclub based on their desire to be integrated. In today's athletic world, there are black, brown, white, and yellow players, some functional and some dysfunctional, with all gradations of ability. The best coaches are able to set boundaries and let athletes know that if you cross a certain boundary you are messing with the team. And no individual is greater than the sum of the parts."

House continues: "There is always a certain percentage of your guys that are high maintenance, a certain percentage where you only have to tell them once, and the ones in the middle who can be influenced by either end. What you have to do is put boundaries around the guys that cause you problems, support the ones that won't cause you problems, and make sure the rest of the herd follows where you want the herd to go."

This awareness comes with letting the team be the team within the covenant set forth at the start of the year, within team policy. And it depends on the maturity of the team. A high school team will likely need more structure than a major league team, and a team with few veterans may, likewise, need more direction and prodding. But, if you have enough veterans who can lead by example and will stand up when someone strays the course, letting them exhibit their own personality can be beneficial.

Promoting autonomy is like teaching. The best teachers don't actually teach, they get the child to learn because teaching can be biased and limited to the ideas of the teacher and the textbook, but learning is virtually limitless.

Tom Trebelhorn likes to let his players express their personalities, to feel free to be who they are: "I've not yelled or screamed much in my career, but I think I've set a pretty good, hard-working, organized tone which allowed players freedom within the system to express themselves as players. As a result, I think whenever the players have an environment where they can express themselves freely, they're self-motivated. I try to clear the path so they can be self-motivated, so there aren't many other factors that block that motivation or make them think about other things."

One of the biggest challenges with giving players autonomy is making sure they stay within the boundaries set forth in the covenant. That's where the head coach or manager steps in. By giving good athletes, or even star athletes, some freedom, they may not all know where to draw the line. But that's OK. Jim Leyland has seen that. He discusses the type of players he's had on his winning teams: "I've never seen a good player yet that wasn't a little selfish. I think real good players in my opinion are a little bit selfish. What I mean by that is they want to be up there, they want to be the guy. A lot of guys need to be that guy. You want selfish players but yet you want unselfish players. So, I think you have to have a little bit of that in you if you're going to be a real good player, a championship player."

So, in giving some freedom of expression to "selfish" guys, they just need to be kept in check somewhat. Giving players some leeway in how they go about their business is one way of developing the chemistry of the team. It's letting their energy flourish.

Controlling the Atmosphere

Allowing good teams that may be inclined to become arrogant the liberty to express themselves means they need to be monitored. Many ways exist for a coach to monitor the team, control the atmosphere, and provide a winning environment.

Controlling the atmosphere is about getting each player to the proper mental state to perform at his best, and getting the team to feel each other's preparedness. Sometimes the coach may have to pull the reigns in a little bit, get the players back on course or remind them of the covenant. Ideally, they are reminded of the covenant every day anyway. They know what's expected of them by the encouragement of the coaches, the motivational atmosphere of the locker room, and the positive reinforcement when things are tough.

During the game, controlling the atmosphere is one of the most important things a coach can do. When things are tense, the crowd is roaring, and everything is crazy, the players will look to the coach to see his response. Players will subconsciously mimic his response to the situation. If he's pacing, swearing, and acting tense, it will transfer to the players. However, if he's confident, reassuring, and in control, the players will sense that too, and they can project that same mood, easing the way for their skills to take over.

Terry Francona tries to control his temperament in the dugout: "If a player messes up and you want to yell, if it's not going to help that player, if you're yelling to help yourself because you're pissed, you can't yell. You have to suck it up and hold on because it isn't going to do anybody any good. The player's coming off the field, he's mad, you're mad, so you go yell at him, and both of you are mad, nothing helps. If you wait until the next morning, and you say, 'Hey, what were you doing?' You're not pissed anymore, he says he messed up. Well, he learned from it. Because that's what you want. You want you're players to learn from their mistakes, rather than having confrontation after confrontation, and nothing gets solved. It's hard to do sometimes. When you're pissed, that's when you have to suck it up, deal with it later when emotions are out of it."

Jim Leyland has won championships because of his leadership. He knows how to get the most from his players. Leyland explains: "My most important role is controlling the atmosphere a little bit. And making sure they're ready to play, making sure they know and are ready for situations that may come up during the game." Controlling the atmosphere involves putting the players in an atmosphere conducive to winning: one that's focused, intense, calm, ready, positive, and proactive.

Continual positive reinforcement is one way to control the atmosphere, and monitor the energy of the team. Tom Trebelhorn explains: "I try to get the players to feel good about themselves, and to keep distractions away from them, other than the distractions they face in trying to hit the pitcher, field a groundball, or throw a strike. I try to be a buffer for all the other stuff."

And distractions are plentiful that will confront baseball players: drugs, alcohol, girls and parties, the media, whatever. It's easy to become distracted and lose the focus essential for winning.

"I try to get the clubhouse going well, try to keep the media in line, try to diffuse any problems that might be happening between players, or between players and front office or fans, or whatever it might be. Then when it comes time, make the correct decisions during the course of the game to put the club in the best position possible to win. Whether it's a pinch hitter, relief pitcher, defensive alignment, hit-and-run, stealing a base, whatever it might be," Trebelhorn explains.

Developing Team Unity

When many pieces of wood are glued together the right way, they become stronger than one single piece. They fit together to become stronger than when standing alone. Chemistry is the same way. Getting players to buy into the team concept can be difficult at times, especially in professional baseball. Players often come from varied backgrounds, cultures, and ethnic groups. To get them all to pull the rope in the same direction may take some effort on the part of the manager.

Rod Delmonico addresses this issue with his players: "We talk about it. You might not like somebody here but you have to accept him. We won't have any cliques. For me, I don't have Tennessee kids, Florida kids, Latin kids—we're all a team. I don't let those cliques go. I'll tell our Latin kids, 'You hang with somebody else besides kids from Miami.' And I'll tell our Tennessee kids, 'You hang with somebody besides Tennessee.' Team chemistry is huge. You can't have a bunch of individuals. I'll tell our guys, 'We got one guy out, he's out in a boat by himself. We either got to get him in here or get rid of him.' I'll tell the kid, 'Either you come in, be a part of the team, or you get the heck out of here.' But I'll challenge our kids, we've got to bring him in, we're pretty good with him. We got to keep chiseling away, get him into the team concept."

One of the ways to get players to respect and accept other players is to understand where they're coming from. For example, a player from Latin America coming to play in the states is entering a totally new culture. What is friendly in his culture might be rude in American culture, and vice versa. But if players don't know that, they might mistake a friendly gesture for something else.

Teambuilding can also be done by educating the guys from one culture about another culture. For instance, a team may be racially divided (i.e., the South African Olympic team, or a team in the deep South), and yet they learn to respect other races by watching a documentary or listening to a guest speaker.

Another way to build team unity is through the use of a superordinate goal. Psychologist Muzafer Sherif used the term "superordinate goal" in a psychology experiment examining intergroup conflict and harmony. A superordinate goal is a goal that has compelling appeal for two groups but which neither could achieve without the other.[2] He found that establishing harmony in a group was most notable when a superordinate goal was set. It could mean bringing Caucasians and Latinos together, or pitchers and position players, for instance. Working through challenging circumstances, and helping players achieve a common goal off the field may also help them on the field.

That is the philosophy behind companies sending their employees on weekend excursions in the woods (such as Outward Bound[3])—to develop teamwork, experience some tough physical challenges, and to learn to lean on and trust each other. Such excursions present great opportunities for developing superordinate goals.

Terry Francona agrees that going through battle together brings about this sort of camaraderie: "Loyalty, team unity—everyone wants that, and everyone strives for that, but you have to go through things, and live through things; you can't force it. That's why I feel better coming in this year, because we have a year under our belt of going through what we went through last year, and we'll be closer for that. The players know that I won't turn my back on them, and I know that they'll battle. So, already we have an advantage going in to this year."

Ed Cheff incorporates a lot of off-field activities to bring his players together as a team, and, through it, he gets close to his players: "We're real close to them, we do a lot of things off the field. We go skiing together, we do the firewood project together where I saw the logs and they chop them. It's a fundraiser; we get a bunch of logs donated and we cut them up with chainsaws, and the players split it and throw it on a truck. We sell it and make about $12,000-14,000 on the project. They work three weekends a year doing it in November—each guy has to work three weekends. So, it's kind of a fundraising type thing but a team deal, you want to go to Hawaii, you have to earn your own money, earn the way to go." Cheff's players work together in order for everyone to get to Hawaii. That is a perfect example of bringing people together, who may not all be friends, and getting them to work together to achieve a common goal.

Rod Delmonico does a lot to bring his teams together also: "We really emphasize that we're a team, a family. We'll take them horseback riding as a group, we'll have a cookout, we'll play basketball as a group, have a ping-pong tournament. Probably 18-20 of our guys will go to our football games together. They go to movies together, they go out. We do that as much as we can, get them together for team breakfasts, things like that."

Another way to enhance team unity is to be honest and true to your word. Mike Hargrove explains: "I think you have to demonstrate loyalty. I think that my players know I appreciate their loyalty and they know that I'm going to be loyal back to them."

Hargrove continues: "That develops a lot of team unity because nobody's ever guessing where somebody else is coming from. You know pretty much where you're coming from, where you stand, and you can relax and trust each other. That's what team unity is, it's just trusting your friend."

Deep down players want to get along with each other; they want their teammates to be their friends. However, sometimes they don't know how to do it within their personality and competitive nature. They want to be cool, they want to be good, and they want to win. They also want friends, but sometimes they aren't sure how to temper their competitive spirit with the desire for friendship. Skip Bertman explains: "Players want to be good teammates, but often competition pulls them toward goals that are self-serving."

As stated before, baseball is an individual sport played in a team format. To be good at it, players need to spend time on their own, whether it's doing mental training or hitting off a tee. They need to push distractions aside, even if it means missing out on fun times with friends. Friends don't always understand the amount of effort it takes to realize the greatness the player is shooting for. So, they get used to pushing people aside to work on their own thing. They need a coach to help them learn how to be a good teammate and to understand the value of team unity.

Larry Dierker tries to develop a certain attitude on the team: "You have to develop some sort of *esprit de corps* as a team. You have to have guys that get along with each other and like to come to the ballpark. Guys that work together and have some sort of synergy going, where if one guy fails in a situation, he feels like another guy will pick him up. It's teamwork, that type of thing. And teamwork comes with guys liking each other."

Players have a greater chance of becoming friends if they have a positive atmosphere to come to, and they have a common purpose, a big goal. Mike Hargrove tries to maintain an upbeat atmosphere: "I try to keep a good positive atmosphere in the clubhouse and on the ball club where the people believe in you and each other."

Building a Family Atmosphere

To go one step beyond creating a positive atmosphere would be trying to create a family-type atmosphere. A family that functions well is honest with each other, willing to work together, and capable of agreeing upon common values. They form a team and make everyone feel like they are an important part. They won't always agree, but they will have enough respect for each other to put the disagreement aside for the common good.

Pat Gillick describes his approach: "Our philosophy is teamwork and family. To be successful requires more than one person, it requires a group of people. So for our organization, the emphasis is on teamwork, working together, and communication. I think that's the only way you can be successful. One person cannot control everything. There has to be delegation of responsibility.

"What we try to do is let everyone have input in any decision we make involving any of our players. I think over a period of time everyone feels included, everyone feels a part, and knows that they'll be called upon and counted upon for their opinion in what we do in the organization," Gillick continues.

Brian Sabean, general manager for the San Francisco Giants, does the same thing: "I think if you involve the people around you in the decision-making process, when it comes time for a tough decision, they'll have more respect for you. Now, at the end of the day, I've got to live with what we decide to do. But it makes it easier for everybody to stay on the same page. While you might not agree with what we're doing, you've had a chance to voice your opinion; so, there's very little second-guessing. That doesn't happen overnight." For coaches, it means keeping all 25 players involved and using them according to their roles. This makes everyone feel they are a vital part of the team.

Getting the team to work together, to have a family atmosphere, is what Bob Bennett tries to do: "The biggest things needed to build a championship team are commitment and togetherness. That's the most challenging part about coaching, but also the most gratifying—developing a team. It's relatively easy to give out information, but it's another thing to coach. And it's another matter to take all that coaching and connect, making the team play as one."

During such a long season players will disagree. Even families who love each other will have a flare-up occasionally. Dusty Baker explains it well: "Basically, it is like my brother and me, it is OK for us not to get along sometimes, but nobody else better touch it. I invite competition from within, with each other, but I don't want to see the signs of envy or jealousy. At the same time, we're going to work, we want to have some humor and some fun, as long as it's not distracting, and to realize what our goal is: "Play ball, play together, and win."

Kevin Towers knows that bringing players together on a baseball team is essential: "One hundred sixty-two games is a long schedule. Your family is those guys in the clubhouse. The closer you can get to those guys or the more you alienate yourself from them, the longer it's going to be, and the more difficult it's going to be. So we try, at least from the management side of things, to do as many things as we can during the season to bring these guys together when time allows. During spring training, we put events together that are going to bring them closer together, and, hopefully, make the season not so long."

Embracing Change

One of the biggest aspects of being successful in any field is being able to adapt. It's been said that the only constant is change, and that is so true. Those who are able to adapt to the changes are those who are successful. Hitters have to adapt to a changing count during their at-bat. They have to adapt to pitchers who throw hard or slow, to umpires with different strike zones, and to numerous other things. Pitchers have to do the same thing, and so do managers.

To maintain the desired chemistry and atmosphere on the team, the manager has to adapt to change. The team's win/loss record will change every game, and he must adapt to the different moods from this. Some players may go into a slump, some may get injured, or a number of other things will happen that need adjustments. These circumstances can all affect the chemistry of the club.

College coaches experience some major changes in their players as they go through four years of growing, learning, absorbing. A bright-eyed freshman will come onto campus in awe of the facilities, the upper classmen, the girls, etc. After he has a few years under his belt, suddenly he's the BMOC (big man on campus). Like a butterfly, he has transformed from a skinny kid from Schenectady, to the Pac-10 player of the year. It could happen.

Players are never today what they will be tomorrow. Who they are, their complete physical and mental being, adds up to much less than their potential. The great coaches see this in their minds and imprint it in their players' minds. And they constantly adapt by staying one step ahead of their players. They see the changes that are coming (the improvements and the failures), and they prepare to deal with them.

Jim Dietz talks about molding young players: "A freshman may have one set of goals, but by the time he's a sophomore, he's going to a have a different set. And that same freshman who was so innocent, starts thinking of nothing else but the draft. He goes from the best kid in the world to work with to a real head case by the time he's a junior because his mom and dad are discussing his millions of dollars they think he's going to make. So there will be stages in these young kids' lives and your team chemistry changes.

"Players change every year, every month, every week, and can change every day, so you have to be alert to this as you go through it. That is probably the hardest thing about coaching and developing continuity. Being aware of when that's going to happen and trying to learn how to deal with it because there are no textbooks—coaches have to be aware that these things change.

"Then you have your outside elements that affect your athletes. It could be health, romance, academics, money, family problems, or family health problems; it could be any multitude of things that affect your athletes during the course of the season. So, all these things have to be factored into coaching and developing players and teams. There is no one easy way because what you left last night could be changing at 9:30 the next morning. So, in coaching, there is no one easy way to develop a winning chemistry. There are a multitude of things, probably thousands of things, that factor into this," Dietz continues.

Harness the Energy

Phil Garner has a detailed approach to coaching, and to discipline. He wants players who toe the line and are conscientious and put the team first. Yet he also likes a mix of guys who maybe toe their own lines sometimes, guys who are somewhat independent. He doesn't temper that independence without rules however: "Damn right you have rules. And discipline is a major portion of it. Without discipline, without standing up to some of these players, the ballclub falls apart. You have to have managers that are willing to step out, when a player's stepped out of line, you have to call a player on the carpet. Discipline, or lack of it, the lack of facing disciplinary action for individual players, will rip apart a good team quicker than anything. It will destroy the morale of a ball club quicker than anything."

Garner continues: "So, you see, we're playing with fire. On the one hand, I want the players that will force me to discipline them. If I have players that I don't have to discipline, I'm not going to win; I promise you. If they all toe the line and they're all really good, the umpire may call strike three and the ball's so far outside, but the player puts his hat in his pocket and walks off. And the other pitcher's throwing at them and knocking them on their ass and they don't ever say a word—they get up and dust themselves off; tough plays at second base, and they just run off the field, don't say a word... You give me those players, they're nice to manage, but you won't win. Give me players that require discipline that I've got to force to toe the line once in a while, I'll win. Any manager will.

"So, you want players that push the envelope, but you've got to have a disciplinary system, and you've got to be willing to use it if you're going to succeed. Because what happens is, there has to be an authority figure, and he has to exhibit authority. If he fails to do that, he won't have everybody in the same direction. If everybody is heading off in different areas, the manager has to pull them back or push them forward. If he doesn't do that, those infractions keep going and you get a lost cause," Garner elaborates.

Principle #4
Create Team Chemistry

If a common theme exists on championship teams, it's energy within the team—an intensity and competitive fire, which equates to players pushing each other and inspiring each other. To get this energy, players have to put the team first. If they do that, regardless of how they get along off the field, they can win.

To get players to put the team first, communication must be very clear and open. They need to know their responsibilities and individual roles. (The covenant helps with this). Then they need the opportunity to fulfill those roles—especially the players on the bench who are vital to the success of the team. Even the very last player should know his importance.

Players should also have some freedom to express themselves, as long as they stay within the boundaries of the team. It's OK for players to be a little cocky. In fact, the great ones tend to have some degree of cockiness in them anyway. That cockiness may lead to some friction among team members, but that's part of that energy.

Team unity is enhanced when players go through things together. Having superordinate goals is one way to achieve this—community projects, for example. Working hard together is another way to build team unity, by sharing a mutual experience. When players go through something really challenging, they form a common bond.

When players go through difficult challenges, certain players will step up. These leaders play a critical role on the team by pushing and policing the other players, and motivating them to compete. This, in turn, stimulates the energy, and produces a team that people say has chemistry.

CHAPTER 5

Coach the Details

"Our philosophy is to coach detail. We feel like if we can coach the details, then the big picture takes care of itself. When players get into game situations (when the game's on the line), they execute. Players that haven't been coached in detail have a tendency to panic or not know what they are supposed to be doing."

— Phil Garner
Manager,
Milwaukee Brewers, Detroit Tigers

During any sporting event, certain things may get overlooked, even by someone who is a student of the game. This is especially true in baseball. It's a game with a fairly leisurely pace, mixed with some high intensity, split-second plays that can mean the difference between winning and losing.

All aspects of baseball, including split-second plays, are comprised of four main areas: hitting, throwing, running, and fielding. How skillfully each team does those four things determines which team wins. Mastering these fundamentals takes careful preparation, not only on the field, but also in the classroom.

That means players need some cognitive ability, to not only know what to do in any given situation, but also how to position their body instinctively and immediately to execute the play. This enables them to succeed where others fail by eliminating one step in the process, the split-second hesitation before a player gets his body in the proper position, and then carries out the play.

Those who know the game well can make the game less complicated by eliminating some variables. They also know that they must excel in situations that come up repeatedly during games, such as the 6-4-3 double play (i.e., the shortstop fields a ground ball, he throws to the second baseman who tags second, who then throws to the first baseman who tags first).

The coach who knows his players well can put them in the position where they are most likely to succeed. With careful preparation and attention to the details of the game, he can build a team that possesses the focus and discipline to excel in the heat of battle.

Plan and Prepare

Just like a general precedes a battle with a plan of attack, a championship coach takes his philosophy and establishes the goal, along with an exact plan and a mode of operation to achieve it. Whatever the goal, if it's worthwhile, then it requires detailed preparation. That involves defining the mission, making the blueprints, assigning the most important parts to be executed over and over until they're almost mindless, and then doing it.

Jerry Kindall was adamant that his practices were just as important, or even more so, than the games: "Organization and careful preparation are so important in winning a championship. At Minnesota we would have a practice plan drawn up everyday, with time frame and schedule. From 2:30 to 2:50 we'd do a certain thing, and, when I was a player, I remember how important it was to see my name on the practice plan. That meant he was thinking about me, planning for me.

"[At Arizona] when we started practice, the players could look at the practice plan and see and think that if we do the following things he laid out, we've got a chance. And they bought it. They respected my hours of preparation and my assistant coaches doing the same thing. If we organize, as coaches, we can expect our players to work hard. If we don't organize, small wonder they get fidgety or bored or don't have a good practice. So organization and careful planning is crucial to the success of the team," Kindall explained.

This careful preparation not only gives players a way to visualize their success since they can see how it will be carried out, but it also gives them a mission and a common focus. Gary Adams explains a common characteristic of his best teams: "They have a sense of purpose. They're very well prepared. I used to watch John Wooden's practices and he had an art of organization and preparing his teams. He wasn't so much concerned with how the other team was doing; he was concerned with how his own team was prepared."

Preparation, ultimately, is the key—intelligent preparation of the right things, in the right manner, in the right order. That's a big job, as Tom House illustrates: "You can have all the positive visualization in the world, but unless you are physically and biomechanically prepared, and nutritionally sound, then the mental/emotional management is not going to happen."

All of this preparation is done not only on the practice field, but also continually throughout the day. The team is on the field for roughly three hours a day, and even with intense, proper focus during that time, the player still has 21 hours left to figure out what he's going to do with. Championship teams coach the details, 24-7 (twenty-four hours a day, seven days a week). Players need to be in the mindset of always pursuing the ideals of their covenant and pursuing excellence. This kind of total preparation is what's needed to be ranked among the best.

Terry Collins explains his philosophy: "I really believe that you have to be up-front and honest. You have to have plans, and you have to be organized. There's more to winning by preparing than once the game starts. It's the stuff that gets the players prepared before they get on the field that forms my philosophy."

Jerry Kindall relies on that kind of preparation in his plans: "Our preparation creates a focus and concentration when we are ready to start the game. Like going to war, our armor is on, and our artillery is in place; we don't have to be uneasy that we haven't prepared for this. We know the pitcher; we know his tendencies. We play each other enough in our league so we know our opposition pretty well. We've scouted and prepared our players for that team, we know the ballpark, so we've done our job, fellas. 'Guys we're going to turn you loose now, we've done our best. You've really had great practices, you're ready.' I feel the practices belong to the coaches, the games belong to the players."

When a team has faced every situation imaginable in practice, and they've executed in pressure situations, they gain confidence. They learn to do it again and again and to make it a habit. They become consistent at trying to be as good as they can be every day.

Hargrove talks about how his best teams did this: "The most common element is their consistency and approach to how they do things. Obviously, the talent level is a lot higher in successful places than others, but, more than anything else, it's a consistent approach to how you do business, and, again, not having people sitting around wondering what the heck they're doing [each day]. That allows our players to relax and allows their ability to work for them instead of them trying to make their ability work."

Defense is Crucial

Two critical areas necessary for planning and preparing as a team are throwing and fielding, or, rather, pitching and defense. In baseball, as in most team sports, if the opponent doesn't score, they can't win. Even with the so-called "juiced ball," the old adage remains true, "Good pitching stops good hitting."

Defense can be much more involved than offense in terms of where players should be and what they should be doing. Offensively, players really only have two places to be: in the batter's box, or at a base. The defense, however, has many more variables and is where many championship teams form their advantage—pitching and defense.

Sparky Anderson explains: "If I were going to build a perfect ball club, I would build pitching first. To me, pitching is the number one thing in the game of baseball. Number two is defense. Number three is speed, and number four would be power. Power to me is useless; I have no love for power. It is a useless thing, but pitching, speed, and defense will beat your brains out. If you cannot score and I can run, you're in trouble."

Coaching the details is about getting players to know their assignments inside and out, to be totally prepared, and to be able to execute under pressure when it counts. A position player may only get up to bat four times during the course of a game, but he plays defense all game long.

Jim Lefebvre, former manager for the Seattle Mariners, explains: "To win, you have to play good defense, because pitching and defense give you a chance every day. That's all you ask for. Don't beat yourself. There will be times when you get beat by them, but don't beat yourself. [Championship teams] learn how to play defense; I think defense is the foundation."

Brian Sabean, general manager for the San Francisco Giants, reiterates Lefebvre's words: "If you pitch good and play good defense, it enhances your ability to stay in games so that it comes down to timely hitting. And then we don't have to out-slug anyone, we don't have to rely on two or three guys in the lineup."

Dick Tidrow, Giants director of player personnel, agrees: "If you do not give up many [runs], then each guy on your team believes he has done something good in the course of the year—they all think they are clutch hitters. But if you are in a big battle, heavy runs every day, it really comes down to who your power hitters are. If all of your scores are 7-6, it starts leaning on your bigger hitters more so than if your scores are 2-1. Anybody can be a hero that way.

"Basically you need an abundance of pitching because if the other team does not score many, then almost every hit you get is some kind of a big hit which builds character for your own team. Everybody thinks, 'I tied yesterday's game, I can win today's game.' I think the ball always finds the guys that cannot play defense very well in our game. So, you have to have good defensive players," Tidrow adds.

Master the Fundamentals

Winning on defense means mastering the fundamentals. Jerry Kindall feels that excelling at the fundamentals helps put his teams in championship games. He explains his philosophy: "[To be a champion takes mastering the] fundamentals. As the assistant coach for Dick Siebert at the University of Minnesota, I learned the value of fundamentals. Since we practiced indoors so much because of the bad weather, we took time to do the little things: proper running fundamentals, breaking down the throwing motion into fundamental components. All the baseball skills were approached very systematically: run, throw, hit, and field. The most important emphasis was a constant review and practice of the fundamentals. [That means] hitting the cutoff man, being in the proper position, having the proper body positioning when they fielded a ball, when they threw a ball, and when they were up at the plate. The teams that win in the big leagues have been very careful and proper with fundamentals in spring training and in practice."

Fundamental baseball means focusing on the important details of the primary aspects of the game and executing them during the game. In addition, it means going with the percentages. That's what Kindall did. He explains: "I'm a percentage coach, always have been. We may be going to a foreign field; we may be playing a team we haven't played before. If you have talent on the team, and the players can execute, and we have prepared them in practice, then I'm a percentage coach. I don't do things off the wall or bizarre; there are not a lot of surprise moves. In a bunt situation, if that's the best percentage move to score a run, you can expect us to bunt. Now, we have to execute. The difference comes with having players that were good enough to execute the fundamentals."

Phil Garner illustrates the structure of his detail-oriented philosophy: "By being detailed, we are saying that everything's important and nothing should be overlooked. We try to instill that value. 'Don't overlook anything, know what you are supposed to do and execute when the time comes.'

"Here's an example. The ball's hit down the left field line and most players say, 'I'm the right fielder, I don't have anything to do.' We're saying, 'Be where you're supposed to be.' It could be one play in the course of the year where that ball goes down the line. The guy on first base stumbles, and the left fielder runs down there and picks it up with a play at second base. The right fielder moves in behind the second baseman, the ball kicks away and maybe there was a runner at first base. He picks it up and throws the runner out going to the plate.

"If he does that one time, the left fielder does that one time, the center fielder does that one time, the catcher does something similar to that one time, the next thing you know, you've got seven players on the team that by being where they were supposed to by some silly little detail, we've won seven ball games we shouldn't have won, and that's seven games our opponents won't win on us because we did what we were supposed to do.

"The value here is that we want players to be detail-oriented, we want them to know what they are supposed to do, be there, and be team oriented. We want them to know, 'Hey, if I am doing my job right here, it transfers into the bigger picture which is, it does the job for the team. If I am where I'm supposed to be, then they can't take an extra base on us, and that falls right into the coaching philosophy.'

"We tell them what the objectives are, first and foremost, and then we review it so much so that they know what they're supposed to do every time, and then it becomes second nature to them. So, the first part of the process is a meeting in the morning before each type of those fundamentals. Today was first and third defense plays, so we had a brief meeting to describe what we wanted them to do, verbal chalkboard type. Then we went on the field today and part of the individualistic fundamental session was each player had to work on his footwork.

"The pitchers had an individual session and we were rolling in balls so one player would yell out, 'First base, second base, or third base.' So, he's supposed to put his feet in the right order and get his body in position—that's the detailed coaching which should be second nature. So, when he gets in a situation when it's first and third, then he can concentrate on what he's supposed to do, not on what his body has to do. In other words, if you haven't put a fundamental in that says keep yourself in a good athletic position, then the first thing that happens when he steps off the mound is he's standing straight up. He wheels to throw the ball, he gives you a [poor] throw, and now he panics next time he's in that situation. The individual fundamental session shows them precisely what we want them to do with their feet and their body that puts them in the right position (for first and third defense). One thing they did not have to think about was 'what's my body supposed to do?' the minute he steps off. Every single fundamental is preceded by a basic fundamental on what you do with your body before you are able to address what you are supposed to be doing on the field," Garner explains.

Start in the Classroom

The ability to execute the fundamentals starts in the minds of the players. Each player needs a mental map of the correct actions to take in any given situation, (e.g., what to do in first and third situations, where to throw the ball, which base to back up, etc.). And it can't be a slow, deliberate process; it has to be instinctive. It has to be bam-bam-bam. When a ball is hit down the left field line, everyone has something to do. They need to do it quickly and precisely. This happens when they have cognitive understanding. In other words, they've visualized it mentally, and they've been through it over and over physically.

Garner explains how he does it: "My coaching philosophy starts in a classroom environment where we describe what we're doing with the players, to an individual workout where we kind of walk each player through the system. Then, we try to add a little speed to it, then run it as a team fundamental, and finish off by adding the whole team and going full speed.

"We start off with detail: we talk it, chalkboard it, talk it, walk them through it, explain the fundamentals over and over again, then practice it on an individual basis and then we move it to a team basis adding a little bit of speed, then we reinforce it by even more speed and doing it several times.

"My philosophy is very detailed in that we review it both verbally and physically. We evaluate players based on whether they know what they are supposed to do... not whether they make a physical error or not. Did they know what they're supposed to do? Then, if they didn't know what they were supposed to do, then why didn't they know? If we've covered it right, they should know."

Teaching players in cognitive detail often means more than just taking players into the classroom and drawing it up on the chalkboard. It means imprinting it in their minds. Having a playbook can facilitate that process. Ron Polk is very meticulous in his preparation and coaching. He explains: "Each of our players gets a baseball playbook, that's our manual. It tells them the rules and regulations of the program, it talks about every situation that we may confront, and all our signals offensively and defensively."

Polk continues: "When school starts in the fall, our practices have three purposes: one is to completely evaluate the ball club. At the end of fall ball we finish with player evaluations, and each player makes out a lineup versus left handers and right-handers, and we pass that on to the players. Two is the presentation of our offensive and defensive scheme. Our practices revolve around doing things that are going to happen in the ball game, so when it happens in the game, they get the mental sensation, 'I've been here before.' The 6-4-3 double play, we do over and over again. They feel comfortable because they've been there before, over and over.

"Whether its rundowns, fly ball communication, bunt defense, or signals from the dugout, we try to make it as oriented to the game as we possibly can, game speed. Give them breaks in practice so they don't get physically and mentally fatigued. Make it to the point where every time something happens in a ballgame they say, 'I feel good about it because I've been here before over and over again.'" he explains.

Ed Cheff has his classroom on the field. The chalkboard is the diamond: "We do walk-throughs; we'll go on the field and we'll walk through it. OK, first and thirds [baserunners], these are the types of things the offense can do to you. The guy can vacate early, they can drag, they can push, they can hit and run, they can steal, they can delay steal. Here's what we do: we throw through, we pump, we throw to the cut man. They drag we do this, they push we do this. OK, that's the classroom."

First and third situations are a prime example of the necessity of coaching the details. Since the offense has a number of options, the defense has to know each possibility, and how to respond to it. Cheff illustrates: "A guy vacates [first base] early: step off, pump to third, and get the ball to the shortstop. If there's two outs, the first baseman will trail the runner, and [tag] him before we go to the plate. If there's less than two outs, [the first baseman is] not going to trail; we're going to make the play back at first. With two outs, if the first baseman sits right in the runner's jock, the guy turns around and we tag him out. So, you have to know the difference. We tell them, first and third, any type of delay steal or steal, with two outs we have to chase [the runner on first]. The first baseman's right off his back. If there's less than two outs, we can't afford to do that because I don't want to make the tag and give up the run."

Every infielder has to be very aware of what he has to do in each situation, and what everyone else will do. Therefore, detail coaching is focused primarily on individual actions—reinforcing what each player has to do, and cultivating their ability to have the focus and discipline to do it every time. Garner acknowledges this: "We are more individualistically oriented in the beginning, moving to a team approach in the end." Being individually oriented in the beginning allows a more detailed approach, then the coach can look at the team's actions as a combination of the individual actions.

For this, it's important for a coach to recognize how players learn best, take instruction, and visualize their future successes. Tom House explains: "Inform, instruct and inspire. There's three ways to learn: you can hear, see, and feel. I like to have the actual video with the game sounds going on. The written side of the equation is important, looking at scouting reports, and also having him verbalize it. Having that individual tell you what he's going to do, because thinking it and verbalizing it matches up the two pieces. Then, all you have to do is go out and actualize it. I say, 'See it, feel it, do it.'"

Cognitive Responsibility

Understanding how different players think can help the coach, but, in the end, the player must be able to think for himself on the field if he's going to be successful. Scouts look for that trait, and coaches, by nature, want coachable players—the ones who will improve through listening and applying what they've been taught.

Dusty Baker explains: "What I am looking for in young players is, do they have the ability to learn, to be taught? You start with skill first, and after that, do they have the ability to retain what they're taught, and then, do they have the ability to apply it upon command? That is what I look for in a player."

One of the primary positions cognitive ability is needed is behind the plate. The catcher is the leader on the field, calling out the plays and handling the pitcher. A good catcher can boost a pitcher's confidence level and impact the team in many ways. Dick Tidrow said the best catcher he ever threw to was Thurman Munson of the New York Yankees. The reason? "Baseball intangibles," Tidrow explained. "Knowing who to throw what pitch to, when to repeat pitches to hitters, when to change speeds, how to use a guy's equipment (his pitches) for that given day. If you are a fastball/slider guy, and on a given day when you are warming up, he'd go, obviously this guy doesn't have much of a fastball today so I'm going to pitch away with his fastball. I'm also going to have him throw a lot more sliders even though I know sliders are not his strongest pitch on normal days. He had a way of getting you through a day, an inning, or a batter when you did not have your best stuff."

That kind of leader is indispensable on the field. It takes players who think along with the manager (i.e., what he might do next), and players who are mentally tough amidst the chaos of the game to win a championship.

Rod Dedeaux, with all his national championships, was very detail-oriented and demanded a lot mentally. He explains: "My tastes were simple, all I wanted was perfection. That was what we were striving for. For example, if our guy scores, but you didn't do the right thing to score the guy, you were wrong. Physical mistakes totally go out the window. Don't even consider them for anyone that's trying. But mental mistakes were intolerable."

Mental mistakes can easily cripple a team. One of the most damaging errors is missing a sign from the coach. Here's how Ed Cheff deals with it: "It depends on the situation. Has the guy missed a lot of signs before? I don't have a specific thing I do. I've taken a guy out of a game if they miss a sign, especially if they miss it twice in a row. Then, other times I don't make a big deal out of it, if it's not a big thing. Sometimes, it starts to avalanche on them, everybody looks in the dugout. Shoot, he's missed another sign and coach is going crazy. You know, sometimes with guys that I know are trying, I don't do anything. Sometimes, it's better to do nothing—protect a guy a bit. Then, sit down with him before the next game and say, 'Let's go through them again.' [For example], 'Charlie, here they are man. I'm going to give you 50 of them, and you're going to see the steal 50 times, and I have only two ways I do it, and I want you to pick them both up. Now lets go.' Bang-bang-bang-bang-bang. Or, you can stand at first and I'll stand in the third base box and I'll give them to you. If he's stupid, you're more stupid if all you do is yell at him or get pissed off at him. You have to do something to correct it; you have to give him extra time."

Winning in any sport really comes down to physical and mental preparation, and execution. With so many things to think about, focusing those thoughts in the right direction is an important matter. Rod Delmonico explains: "It's a mindset. When you step up to the plate, you have to have a routine that you do every time, some little thing that you do to get you ready, and a mindset of what you're trying to do. You do that before you get in. How is this guy going to pitch me? How is this team going to pitch me? Is it going to be away from my strength? To my strength? How are they going to try to set me up? And then make an approach."

Championship teams make fewer mistakes than the other teams. They can do this because of their thorough attention to detail—they take responsibility cognitively. Phil Garner explains: "[Championship teams] don't make mistakes. They execute when they are supposed to, and execution means: they do it defensively, offensively, and their pitching staff does it too. Their pitching staff is able to make big pitches when they need to. And they constantly stay aggressive."

Aggressiveness stems from practicing and building confidence. When a player has done it over and over successfully, he knows he can do it. Garner explains: "[Winning] comes down to execution; it goes back to the little things. If you can execute the little things when the pressure's on, that's the first part of starting a winning attitude. I can do… It starts with being able to get a bunt down when you have to get a bunt down, or being able to keep a ground ball from going between your legs when there's a runner on third. Keep the ball in front of you if it's a tough hop, so those little things all begin to mount up to where it gives you confidence that you can win."

A key ingredient in winning teams is having players who are mentally sharp. A good coach figures out how to tap into those mental skills that players don't always reveal. They may need help to create a mental image on what to do and how to do it. And techniques will vary depending on how a player thinks. Tom House explains: "Athletes learn by feeling, hearing, or seeing. You can't make a kid that is an auditory learner be visual, and you can't make a kid that is a visual learner be auditory. Conversely, if the kid is a kinesthetic type guy, you can't have him just listening."

Focus on Game Situations

Part of getting players mentally and physically ready to succeed is emphasizing those details that happen most frequently during games. When practice time is limited, especially in college, focusing on game-situations makes practices more efficient.

For Andy Lopez, he simulates game situations with intensity in batting practice. He says, "Drills are very competitive. In batting practice, they take one stroke (on the field) and execute. Now, in the cage, they'll take 10, 15, 20 strokes in a row. But, when they come on the field in a practice setting, they'll take one stroke and get a chance to execute. It's game-like. We'll call out situations. I'll say, 'OK, next three minutes is the inside game (our bunting game); sacrifice, drag, push, squeeze. I'll stand by home plate, and they'll have to call out their skill. So, a batter may say, 'sacrifice bunt', then he's got one chance to execute; either he gets it done or he doesn't. Next guy jumps in he may say 'drag', he has to execute it. Next guy may say, 'push bunt.' Then, we go outside game: hit-and-run, hit-and-run drive (our terminology), important plays like hitting the ball to the right side with a runner on second, nobody out, bases loaded;

hitting the ball out of the infield, runner on third, less than two outs, etc. Then, we'll just go two strike approach for another three minutes. Next, they'll call out any situation for three minutes. We'll do these situations for 15 minutes; it's a very intense, competitive environment, because that's what a game's like. So it's 15 minutes per station. The station before hitting on the field is hitting in the cage.

Ron Polk tries to mimic game situations also: "We don't spend a lot of time on things that happen infrequently during ballgames. We spend a lot of time on repetition of things that happen over and over in a game. I've always been a firm believer that if a player messes up on some type of mental aspect of the game, not being at the right place at the right time, I have to accept as much of the blame as he does, because we haven't emphasized it enough, or covered it enough. But a lack of effort or lack of commitment is his responsibility. It's my responsibility if they don't play well."

One way of emphasizing certain game situations is to point out those crucial things that happen in a game that often get overlooked, and elevate their status. Tom Trebelhorn knows that certain crucial elements of the game are easily overlooked, and statistics are generally not kept, especially for defense. Here's what he does: "I always try to recognize certain things on a game by game system with a plus or minus system. Add those players that didn't necessarily get the hits or home runs or any of that, but they did the little extra things, getting the guy over, getting the sacrifice bunt down, taking an 0-2 count and walking and ending up scoring a run. Trying to bring forth those smaller details within the context of the game that may become overshadowed by a game-winning hit or a three-run homer or a shutout… I try to share the success, and, on the other side, when you're not so successful, also try to point those pivotal and important areas that we broke down. Often times, I'll do that through a statistical breakdown of the game, or a brief note on the board."

Moving a runner from second to third base when there's nobody out is an important detail that doesn't draw newspaper headlines. But, it's an important situation in the game and happens most every game. Garner illustrates: "If a player gets up in the ninth inning, and there's a runner at second base nobody out, and he really tries to shoot the ball the opposite way (toward the second baseman) and he advanced the runner to third, that player had a heck of an at-bat.

"I want to compliment him on that, and that's not going to show up on your salary arbitration, but you did something to help the team win. So, we constantly find ways to commend the player on doing the little things that add up to the big picture. And stats, a lot of the ones we use, are meaningless as far as evaluating a player's performance. So, our constant endeavor is to make players realize what we're looking at, what's important for us."

Eliminate Variables

An essential part of winning is making things simple. Whether it's diagramming the play on the chalkboard or explaining how to hit a curveball, the simpler it can be explained, the better chance the athlete has of understanding it. Not only that, but if an athlete has to spend precious time in thought while reacting, then that may keep him from responding in the exact moment necessary to win the moment. If a batter's got a 2-2 count, and he's thinking he's got to watch out for that pitcher's curve, slider, change, and fastball, he doesn't have much of a chance. Without knowing which pitches he can throw for strikes, the batter is at a disadvantage.

Phil Garner explains how to make things simple. To give athletes the best chance of succeeding: "We eliminate the variables. Baseball is a process of elimination. If you're facing the pitcher, you want to eliminate the pitches he can't throw for strikes. If I tell you that today's pitcher has two fastballs, (a four seam and two seam), a change up, a slider, a curve ball, and a split [-finger fastball], that's six pitches. If you go to the plate and look for one of six pitches, you're screwed. Now, if I tell you this, 'He's got a two seam and a four seam, he can't throw a sinker for a strike, don't worry about it. He's got a slider that curves. He can't throw a curve for strikes, don't even think about it. When he gets into trouble, he's going to go with a fastball, four seam away.' Now, what have we done? We've eliminated all the things he can't throw for strikes, and we've got you zeroed in on what he can throw for strikes, so that's what we try to do."

Eliminating the variables takes a lot of study and careful preparation. Greg Riddoch, former coach with the San Diego Padres, studied hours of film of opposing pitchers every day during the season. "Successful people make a habit of attention to detail. I'm a detail person," Riddoch says. Tony Gwynn says Riddoch's eye for details helped him steal 57 bases in 1987, Riddoch's first season as a Padres coach.[1]

Put Players in a Position to Be Successful

Positioning players to succeed is part of the science of coaching. Knowing who can do what and who will be able to confront and succeed in certain situations is the mark of a championship coach.

Jim Dietz illustrates: "The art of coaching in baseball is trying to know when to take somebody out and when to put somebody in, and getting people to accept roles. There's going to be those who can do certain things and those that can't. So, in coaching, you try to get them in the right place so they can be successful. You have to know your personnel to know what you can and can't do, and how players mature."

Ken Knutson relates: "As a coach, my most important role is to put kids in opportunities where they can have success. You have to see the good and the potential in a kid, and put them in a situation where they can win, and they can have success. That's the most important thing you do. You teach them the game, you get them stronger—all the basic stuff. But, my responsibility is to find out what they do well and put them in [those] situations and then manage the game."

Knutson continues: "Don't expect them to do things they're not capable of doing. Try to get them to do what they do well. See what they do well and enhance that, work with that. If he can't hit the ball the other way, then don't ask the guy to hit the ball the other way. Get a different player to do that. Or, if he's a really good defensive player and he can't hit, then make a role for him. I think we get hung up sometimes, or coaches do, by saying we can change a guy, by coaching him really good, we'll make him something he's not. You should look at a player and see what his strengths are, and use that within the framework of the team or cut him, don't have him around."

Knowing the talent you have and putting those players in positions to be successful involves setting up the proper matchups, predicting the way the game will likely unfold, and implementing personnel most effectively. It helps to know the tendencies of the other team and how they implement their personnel also.

Dierker explains: "The main thing is to try to have a concept going in before the game of what kind of matchups you want. Which hitters will perform against which pitchers, and which pitchers you want to go against certain hitters on the other team. You try to take advantage of statistical information you have and athletic tendencies and traits that you observe. So you can try to put your players in a position where they are likely to succeed."

Essentially, if the players are adept at the fundamentals, know exactly when and where they have to be, and understand how to position their body, then they are preparing well. Terry Collins explains how the good teams do that: "[Winning teams] do all the little things right. They execute the little parts of the game better than the other teams. I think if you had to look at one organization, look at the Atlanta Braves. They're very, very good; they don't beat themselves. Their pitching staff has a game plan and they execute it. Their lineup just doesn't make very many mistakes. If you have to move a runner along, they move him along. Whether it's McGriff, Klesko, or Chipper Jones, they get the guy over. When Maddux is pitching, what he does is say, 'OK, here's what I have to do in this situation, and takes his chances.' He says, 'I need a ground ball here.' He makes the pitches he needs to get a ground ball. So, those characteristics about the Braves, the Yankees… [When] the Yankees hit-and-run, they put the ball in play, they don't swing and miss. All the good teams play the little part of the game."

Principle #5
Coach the Details

To win championships, teams need to execute on a daily basis. The coaching staff has to be organized and prepared with a clear daily plan. Fundamental aspects of the game such as bunting, executing hit-and-runs, turning double plays, backing up bases, hitting the cut-off man, and getting in an athletic position to make a play should be performed flawlessly.

Fundamentals start in the classroom. Players need to be able to see it in their minds before they can accomplish it. The classroom can start with a playbook, a chalkboard, or a drawing in the dirt—whatever it takes to create a mental map of what needs to be carried out on the field.

To imprint this mental map, visualizing themselves executing tasks perfectly is crucial; they need to see everything that can happen in a situation and know what to do. Having cognitive responsibility correlates to a player reducing mental mistakes by gaining the belief that he can confront any situation and flawlessly execute the play.

This is enhanced by going over again and again on the field in practice, those plays that will happen most frequently during games. Practices should mimic game situations as much as possible, to allow players to get a feel for how certain situations will play out in the game. Consequently, they will be prepared for what may come up.

To enhance preparation and confidence, coaches should make the game as simple as possible in the players' minds. This can be done by eliminating variables that are least likely to happen, and focusing on the most likely.

Players become much more confident when they know the coach will put them in the best possible position to be successful. He can do this by analyzing the skills of his personnel, and preparing them accordingly. This kind of attention to detail, allows players to execute the little things that win games without having to think too much, especially amidst the chaos of a close game—they just do it.

CHAPTER 6

Win the Pitch: Setting Goals

"Our goal is to win the next pitch. I want to win every game I've ever coached, no doubt about it. But, I'm more concerned with playing well, and my guys' brains, how they're working—our effort, our character, and our heart...those types of things. The wins take care of themselves."

— Ken Knutson
University of Washington

Winning an athletic event may have more to do with what took place before the game, on and off the field, than the time between the lines. Players have intense practices, prepare themselves mentally, learn to deal with failure, and develop teamwork—all for a few hours of game time. The fans come to see the action on the field, but what champions do to win is a far more detailed thing.

It's a detailed process of seeking excellence. Those who excel know that the road is often long, and with it are many failures. But, rather than getting down, they embrace it as a natural part of winning. In fact, they know they are winners already because they live and practice as if they already are the champions they want to be.

Champions compete against themselves and the game. They realize their biggest challenge is fighting negativity when things go wrong, and the doubts and fear of failure that come with it. They also learn to stay within themselves, by not trying to do too much.

Some champions write down their long-range goals (i.e. winning 50 games, winning a national championship), some verbalize their goals, and some never mention goals at all. Regardless, they all have one overriding pursuit—continually striving for excellence.

Winning in baseball, for the great teams, means achieving excellence every day. Winning teams have players who are able to stay in the moment and make the most of each moment in practice, every at-bat, and even every pitch. It comes down to a goal of winning each pitch, staying in the moment, and allowing all the work, the visualization, and the preparation to come to fruition.

Be the Champion First

Before a team wins a national championship, they have to play like champions. They must execute the details and be fundamentally sound, play together, push each other, and overcome adversity. For this to happen, each player has to start thinking like a champion, and behave as if he already is a champion.

Champions have a certain chemistry that people notice without having to look at a score sheet or pedigree. It's in the way they walk, the way they talk, and the way they handle adversity. Watch anyone who is the best at something and see how they react to setbacks. It's almost as if they forget about them as soon as they happen. They move on and continue pursuing excellence because of who they are, rather than dwelling on their current situation.

Champions recognize that setbacks are only temporary. Knowing this, they not only take risks when failure is likely, but they also embrace failure as a way toward becoming the person or player they visualize themselves as.

Motivational speaker Warren Bennis says that when film producer Sydney Pollock produced his first film, he wasn't too sure what he was doing. But what he could do and certainly did was act *as if* he knew what he was doing—*as if* he was already a top producer. He watched how other top producers acted, and [he] walked liked they walked, talked like they talked, dressed like they dressed. He produced like they produced.[1]

Gary Adams maintains that acting like a champion precedes becoming a champion: "Every year we start saying our goal is to win the national championship; but, it's going to be one step at a time. I don't believe that you become a champion first and then start acting and training like one. First of all, work and act and train like a champion, then you become a champion. It's a day-by-day process."

Pursuit of Excellence

Acting like a champion is an all-the-time concept as much as daily training. No distinction should exist between practices and games, except that maybe practices have a bit more pressure. Champions pursue excellence in every endeavor and don't really discern between weekends and weekdays—there are no off days from excellence.

To be successful, excellence has to become a part of a player's character. Who they are, how they view themselves, and what kind of teammate they are all contribute to excellence and success. Success comes from being conscientious of the things that define character such as integrity, perseverance, hard work, dedication, and compassion to name just a few.

Bob Todd elaborates: "Success is defined as self-satisfaction that you have done everything you can to be the best you can be. That can lead down that avenue of life, as a coach, a spouse, the best dad... Then players have to have the same maturity level to understand what they're doing: lifting weights, going to bed early and having the proper diet, taking the extra ground balls and doing the extra work—the proper work ethic. All of that goes into play in allowing you to become as good as you possibly can. If the athlete can look himself in the mirror and say he did all that, then you opened up another avenue for the athlete to look at himself and say he didn't lose the game. The other team was just better today. The media has sort of created all this [focus on winning and losing]. It's just the hype and everything else."

Win the Contest With Yourself

Giving 100% every day, every moment means staying focused on the task at hand and not getting distracted by external things (winning and losing, for example), which lead to things such as nervousness, lack of concentration, and muscle tightness. Focusing on the task at hand is a difficult task for the hitter when the crowd is going crazy, the stadium's rocking, and the pitcher is throwing BB's (baseballs that appear to be the size of a BB pellet).

So many factors are present in baseball that a player can't control; focusing on what he can control empowers him. A hitter may hit the ball hard every at-bat, but right at somebody. A pitcher may pitch his best game but lose on a broken bat Texas-leaguer to the ninth hitter in the lineup. He can't control those things, but he can control his effort, his emotions, and his focus, which is one of the most challenging tasks in any sport. Rarely can a player maintain the same intensity from start to finish, as well as control his emotions and focus. When a player can control those three things, he has won half the battle.

Psychologist James Loehr puts it well: "The world's top athletes almost universally agree on one thing: You will always be your own toughest opponent. Until you can conquer yourself, very little is possible against an opponent."[2] Loehr suggests athletes have internal goals for each performance such as to 'win the match with yourself.' If you can answer "yes" to each of the following three statements at the end of play or practice, Loehr states, you have won the most important contest:

1. I gave my best effort every moment. I gave 100 percent.
2. I maintained a predominantly positive, healthy and optimistic attitude with myself.

3. I accepted full responsibility for me today, for what I did and didn't do (didn't blame parents, weather, bad equipment, cheating opponent, or anything else.)

Winning the contest with the self eliminates the external focus and the self-doubt that comes with it. It takes away the "pressure" of performance and one simply performs.

Psychologist Tom House talks about the importance of focusing on what a player can control: "Winning and losing is extremely important, especially when you are getting paid to do it, but that is an external benchmark. You can do everything you are supposed to do as an athlete and still come up with a loss. Conversely, you can do nine out of ten things wrong, and on a given day, with luck, win a game. The winning and the losing are the external benchmark: The internal benchmark: did I prepare myself, did I do what I was supposed to do based on that preparation? In the long run, those athletes will win more than they will lose. So, don't let short term wins and losses, external benchmarks, affect your gratification process."

Setting internal goals around playing hard and staying focused mentally are extremely important. Loehr says that the correct emotional response to a problem is 75% of the solution.[3] The baseball season is so long that getting too emotional can really affect performance—especially in a sport where failure plays a big part in every game.

Process-Oriented Goals

National champion Andy Lopez only sets process-oriented goals. He elaborates: "We don't really set goals per se, we just set a goal to get better each day. Right before practice starts, every day, I tell them, 'let's get better today.' And I'll grade them every day after practice. 'Fellas, today was about a B, or today was a C. It was an average day for you guys. We've got to be better tomorrow.'

"For me personally, I try to get to four players a day, affect four players a day. It might be just, 'How's your girl,' or 'How's your mom,' or 'How's your class?' In the morning, I'll go through my roster and pick out four guys, look at who's going good and who's not, and talk to them. If a guy's going good I'll tell him, and I'll tell him to write it down—how he's feeling, what he's been doing. I tell all of my guys to have notebooks. 'File it, because it might not be going good in two weeks and you'll be able to refer back to when it was going good.'"

Process-oriented goals can help players deal with the game's inherent failure and also help them stay on track. For example, a hitter's goal may be to show up early for the next week and hit 100 curve balls off the machine a day, or take 100 ground balls a day. These are things he can control that are part of the process of achieving the big goal, things that allow the athlete to win the contest with himself. If that hitter gets to the park early, takes his extra 100 swings, hustles around everywhere, plays hard on defense, and still goes 0-4, then he can still feel like he accomplished his goal for that day.

Goals that are internal and process-oriented allow the athlete and team to "win" each day. Oftentimes, players get caught up in the win/lose aspect of competition (i.e., we win/you lose or vice versa)—the zero sum theory. This theory states that if someone has, then someone else has not. In other words, if one team wins another loses, which is not necessarily the case. One team may play poorly, make mental mistakes, and neglect the little things and still win on a broken bat Texas leaguer. The other team may get a clutch hit from its nine hitter who's been in a big slump. Then, he's feeling better about himself and he's more prepared for that next big at-bat down the road. Maybe the losing pitcher pitched an awesome game and learned how to control his emotions with the bases loaded. The team may have come together and rallied around each other building team chemistry. There may be a lot of "wins" that don't show up on the scoreboard.

Ken Knutson looks to win those internal battles more than anything else: "I talk about accountability and work ethic, learning how to play the game, respecting the game, playing against the game itself, those types of things."

Block out the Armchair Quarterbacks

One of the big challenges with maintaining the proper focus is handling the whole slew of people watching the team who play "armchair quarterback." They are the ones who tell players, coaches, and anyone who'll listen, what the team should be doing, how they should be doing it, what's wrong, what's right, and the list goes on. These armchair quarterbacks could be parents, siblings, cousins, friends, and, last but not least, the media. These folks can be called "the armchair team." This team of people fills players' minds with all kinds of things that take them away from their moment-to-moment focus.

They observe and talk about the surface parts of the game preferring to zoom in on and blow out of proportion certain parts of the game such as the home run, the stolen base, the brush-back pitch, things like that. Armchair quarterbacks, as a whole, don't care about character in baseball, nor do they know what it takes to win. They're good at things like talking about how far a home run was hit, or if so-and-so's going to go in the third or fourth round (in the draft).

The armchair team also has a group mentality. One parent may say how well the team played, another parent will chip in a similar comment, and soon everyone will be thinking the team's just got to show up to win.

A team that's totally focused on excellence has to block out the armchair team and their influence. Reading the papers and speaking to the media needs to be done with a grain of salt. The media often ask questions because they're looking for a specific answer, not necessarily the right answer. They're looking for a story and can't comprehend the intense focus needed to be successful.

Art Howe relates a story of his playing days with the Pirates: "To have a championship club, you need leaders on your team. When I played for Pittsburgh my first year in the big leagues, Willie Stargell was the leader for the Pirates. Everybody knew it. He did it in subtle ways. Here's an interesting story: He hit a home run in the bottom of the ninth with two outs in Pittsburgh my first year there—a three-run home run to win the game. All the reporters crowded by his locker after the game, saying, 'Hey Willie, what was it like?' all that. I was about the twenty-fifth guy on the roster and I had pinch-hit in about the seventh inning. I walked but didn't score. We didn't do anything; but I walked and kept the inning going. He told the writers, 'You guys should be over there interviewing Art Howe, because, if he hadn't walked in the seventh inning, I don't even come up with two outs in the ninth.' That's the kind of guy he was; he shared everything. He found reasons to make you feel at home. When one of the writers came over and told me that, I was amazed. That was a clutch hit and what did I do, I just got on base. But that's the way he was thinking." Stargell knew the details of the game that allowed the Pirates to win that game.

The media didn't know or care about anything but the home run at the end. The home run is pushed by the media because that's what the fans like to see. The media doesn't say, "Let's figure out all the keys to winning a championship and focus on those." So, it's easy to get caught up in all the hoopla, and Willie Stargell knew that.

Keeping the team focused on what really matters, as Stargell did, is crucial. Tom Trebelhorn uses his point system during the game to emphasize the things he thinks are important that may get overlooked (see chapter five). Some teams use highlight videos of their past successes in things like getting bunts down, blocking balls, backing up bases, executing the hit-and-run, etc. Rod Delmonico shows his team a highlight video of great defensive plays called "Defense Wins" a number of times throughout the season, to keep them focused on the importance of defense. However it's done, the great teams maintain their focus, block out the armchair team, and stay zeroed in on the task.

Players Controlling their Thoughts

Controlling thoughts, especially during competition, is essential to staying in the moment, and performing ultimately in that moment. Thoughts are such a powerful force because they determine how people function. It's pretty tough to get a positive result while thinking a negative thought, and thoughts are generally positive or negative, not neutral.

North Americans are constantly bombarded by pictures, ads, shows, and billboards that are designed to do one thing: control their thoughts. *Chicken Soup for the Soul* author Mark Victor Hanson says, "People living in a fairly large city are subject to 2,700 advertising messages a day."[4] And that's just advertisements, not to mention all the other negative thoughts in the environment.

Not only is the mind infiltrated by thoughts from the environment and other people, but it also plays tricks on the very person it inhabits. It tells lies and tries to fool people into thinking they can't do something. A person's mind knows one thing very well—the individual's failures—and it will take any opportunity to remind them of it.

It takes mental toughness to overcome all the negativity that the mind churns out. And when the game's on the line, and the hitter's facing a pitcher he's 0-12 against, and the crowd's chanting his name, it's tough to block everything out. However, that's what needs to be done, and that could be the most important part of actual game play.

Mental toughness and thought control go hand in hand. Being mentally tough means basically controlling thoughts in such a way so that players become disciplined thinkers with the ability to stay in the moment. It's blocking out negative thoughts when they keep fighting to get in there. That's when the mental toughness comes into play.

If the mind is left to wander during competition, it's inevitable that it will eventually wander to a negative thought. When that happens, players should do something about it. Skip Bertman sometimes has his players wear a rubber band on their wrist. When a negative thought comes, they are to "snap" themselves away from the negative thought. Even mentally shouting, 'stop!' often does the trick. Then refocus on the task at hand.

Ken Knutson talks about what he considers to be the most important aspect of on-the-field play: "It's the power of the brain to be able to break it down into one pitch at a time, to win pitches, to have a good plan, to do it without freaking out, to have control over your environment. To me, controlling your brain is the most important thing you can do. If I can get nine guys focused on each pitch, then I'm going to be fine. Then, I'll compete for a national championship."

For a player to play at the highest level means controlling how he reacts to things emotionally and physically. Every time something happens, the mind is quick to label it bad or good, instead of just moving on. For example, if a player makes an error, he tends to automatically feel bad. Even former Brewers great Paul Molitor said after he commits an error, he loses some concentration and confidence.[5] It is completely natural to react emotionally to a physical event in the environment. However, it doesn't have to be that way; everyone has the choice on how they will to react to anything.

The problem is that when a player is spending all his time reacting to the physical environment, he's basically at the mercy of fate. If he strikes out, he feels bad and starts thinking negative thoughts. If the same hitter gets a hit, he feels good.

When the hitter can stay on an even keel and not react emotionally to environmental distractions, then he can use the power of his mind to create the mental focus he needs to become his greatest self. This is not only important in a game, but also, and sometimes more importantly, in practice. Since there should be more pressure put on the player (by the coach) in practice than in the game, there should be a heightened sense of focus in practice. However, that's often when players lose their focus, and this carries over to the game.

When going on the field and taking ground balls becomes routine, players start thinking about what they're doing on the weekend, or what they're having for dinner, and the focus for that moment is lost.

Knutson illustrates: "Umpires, the weather, the hitter, the other team, girlfriends, whatever, the flavor of the week can come into their brain, and if that gets in there when they're playing, then they're not going to be as effective. It will lead to doubt, it will lead to being insecure. I think the baseball stuff is really easy—teaching a guy to hit. If he can hit, you might not have to teach him anything. You might give him a plan, but the good players are the guys that have a plan mentally, that execute it, that are mentally tough. It's the same thing for me. My definition for mentally tough is just controlling your brain—controlling your brain to think in a positive manner about what you need to do. Cut the plate in half and look for a pitch away; if I can do that, if I see a pitch away and I put a good swing on it, then I'm a successful player."

Don't Fall a Half-day Behind

One of the problems with not living in the moment is that things start to get away from you. Since you're thinking about other things, whatever you're trying to accomplish doesn't get done, or it doesn't get done as well as it should have. Then you start falling behind which causes unnecessary stress.

Bob Todd illustrates how this can happen: "The one thing that I don't want is for them to show up [for practice] and worry about the test they just flunked or the English paper they just turned in and did a terrible job on. Now, they are going to worry about the academic issues of their life during practice and then go back to their apartment or dorm and try to do homework and worry about practice; now, they're not studying and preparing for the next day.

"Consequently, what we're doing is letting baseball affect academics, and the next day letting academics affect baseball. We're a half a day behind. We've got to get it back on track where when you come to baseball practice, you're not worrying about the test you have to take. By the same token, I don't want you sitting around thinking baseball when you should be thinking about the academics you have to take care of."

Goals Vary—Focus Doesn't

If a team is wholly concerned with the process of making each instant as good as it can be, putting out full effort to achieve it's potential, and visualizing it's goal, then the end result will take care of itself. It's like building a foundation: lay out the plans, get the bricks, and focus on laying each brick as precisely as possible. Soon enough, the last brick will be laid, and the mission will be accomplished. The pitfalls come when the focus is taken off the bricks and geared toward the possible problems.

Every championship coach wants his players to have that heightened moment-to-moment focus, they just often go about it in different ways. Some managers never talk about winning, while others are very clear that their goal is to win it all.

As Davey Johnson puts it: "My goals are simple. I always plan on winning, being around for the big prize at the end; I expect that. But I'm patient and sometimes you make little steps. You've got to be kind of relentless; if something needs to be done, nothing should stop you from getting it done."

Dusty Baker, three-time National League Manager of the year for the San Francisco Giants, sets his sights on the top prize: "First thing is to win the World Series; once you win it once, then keep on winning. The goals that I set are for my guys to win and to be proud to be on the Giants. It's a daily thing that you have to stay on top of in order to achieve."

Kevin Towers sets his goals high also. "Our goal every year is to win the World Series—nothing less. I think anytime you set your sights lower than anything but the top, you're in trouble."

Bob Bennett sets his long-term goal as winning it all, and he wants each of his players to have individual goals also: "Every year, our goal is to get to Omaha and win it. Obviously, you're not going to do that every year, but if you give everything you have, then you're a winner whether you win or lose. Then, we want to make short-term goals for each of us. For example, I want to be a starter; I want to make sure I'm playing every day; I want to be one of the best players on the team, or the best third baseman in the conference. You can set individual goals like that. I want to know what those goals are for each player and we want to deal with them."

Champions seem to have a trigger inside them that motivates them to press on when all others waver, to continue pushing toward the goal when others fall by the wayside. This trigger, no doubt, is aided by a clear vision of their goal. It doesn't matter whether the goal is written or imagined, as long as it is definite.

An old legend exists about a monk who took one of his students to the river. He brought him to the water and pushed his head under and held it there. The student started flailing his arms, and finally, the monk let him up. He asked the student, "What were you thinking when you were under the water?" The student replied, "I was thinking about breathing. I wanted to breathe." The monk said, "That's the focus you should have on the path to your dream."

To reach for the ultimate prize may create stress, but the stress can propel championship-type athletes to reach higher. A lofty goal will help motivate players to practice hard in the October rain when the first game is five months away.

At Lewis-Clark State University, head coach Ed Cheff has led his teams to playing in 11 national championships in a row. For Cheff, this was accomplished by taking it one day at a time: "[My goals are] Just kind of day-to-day things, lets have a good practice today. I never talk about long range. I never talk about winning a national championship. It's, 'let's have a good practice,' then the goal is, 'let's have a good game.' When we get today done, then we'll deal with tomorrow."

It could be that champions have that makeup already ingrained in their systems—the makeup which would have them put forth their best effort to be as good as possible every day. This effort creates a momentum that cannot be stopped. New horizons are forged through hard work, determination, and a moment-to-moment focus.

Tom Kelly wants a focused his commitment to playing hard each day. He doesn't expect anything fancy, he just wants his players to come out each day and give it all they have by playing hard and playing up to their potential. No one mentions a win/loss record. He explains: "My only goal is that the guys go out and play hard each and every night. Give me everything they have and play the game to the best of their ability, and if they do that, I'm fine. My goal each day is to prepare the players the best I possibly can, and get them ready to play. If they play the game to the best of their ability, whether we win or lose, I'm going to be relatively happy."

Ron Polk's goals is very straightforward: "My goal is just for each player to do the best he can that particular day in every facet of his life, not only in the classroom but also as a person and a baseball player." The common thread with goal setting from top coaches like Ron Polk is making each day count, shooting for a great day that day. It comes down to making the most of each moment of the day.

One Pitch at a Time

Setting the goal of winning one pitch at a time is an intelligent option because it goes back to excellence—an all-the-time thing. It takes 1.3 seconds, on average, for a pitcher to deliver the ball from the stretch (from his first move until the catcher catches it). Those 1.3 seconds, plus the 4 to 10 seconds following it if the ball is hit, is when the excellence needs to be applied. The excellence that has been accumulating from each moment of the day is taken and applied in those brief moments.

Seattle Mariners first baseman John Olerud is very good at staying in the moment, for that short window of time. When asked how he was able to hit over .400 as college player of the year in 1988, he replied: "I took each at-bat one at a time. I tried to make each at-bat a good one. And I was just able to continue that throughout the year." Olerud didn't worry about getting out. He just did his best each time.

Being present-focused during a game means doing everything necessary to prepare for the next pitch. It means fielders clearing their minds, previewing possible scenarios, seeing themselves making the play, and then, getting in the ready position and expecting a tough play. It means hitters preparing mentally, blocking out all distractions, and having a plan.

The ability to win the pitch comes partly from doing one's homework. Here's a sample thought process for a shortstop: "OK, this is their leadoff hitter. I know the third baseman will be playing in, looking for the drag bunt. So, I'm ready to cover more ground to my right. And he's hit the ball hard to my right in the past so I'm going to cheat that way a bit and visualize making that diving play to my right. He's also got some wheels, so I'm also going to have to scramble to my feet and throw him out by half a step."

Thus, half the work on winning the pitch comes before the pitch. It's the physical and mental preparation done throughout the fall to get to this point, and the mental preparation done for 30 seconds before he hits that prepares players.

At Washington, Knutson aims primarily for this type of thinking: "We set goals to try to win pitches, win outs, and win at-bats. Don't worry about the score. As far as our approach goes and our effort goes, if we're down by 10 or up by 10, we should still be playing the same game, have the same intensity or potential for a good inning or whatever it is…we've gotten to the point where the thing we're trying to do is win a pitch."

When players work as hard as they can with the moment at hand, win each pitch as Knutson would say, then horizons open up to unknown territories. In other words, nine-hole hitters get game-winning hits, end-of-the-bench players come off the bench in the championship game and make game-saving defensive plays; first year players play like veterans; players play together; they win when it looks hopeless.

A competitive fire burns inside championship-type players. These players are leaders who push each other and make sure what needs to get done gets done. They are the players who realize that the opponent is much more than the other team; the opponent is himself, the game, the other team and all the negative thoughts that will come.

Principle #6
Win the Pitch

Baseball is a game stacked with failure. In a long season filled with ups and downs, if a player doesn't understand and respect the game, he won't be able to master it. A player may do everything right, and still fail. The best players don't look at their performance as a win/lose sort of thing—there's too much failure in the game for that.

Although they may set goals to win the championship or win a certain amount of games, champions make their focus much more detail-oriented than that. Instead of focusing on end results (i.e., winning and losing), they learn to focus on internal benchmarks, such as playing against the game, and winning the contest with themselves.

That contest is much more viable, and can produce optimum results. The goal is a continual pursuit of excellence which means training and acting like a champion on and off the field. Champions are process-oriented and continually work on self-improvement, in every single moment and with every single pitch. They have a heightened moment-to-moment focus, and that is their goal, in practice and in games.

CHAPTER 7

Practice Under Pressure

"I always kept them under pressure in practice, whatever we were doing, so it wasn't anything new. When the pressure was on, I expected them to be performing up to their ultimate all the time anyway. I think that they felt they were better prepared. I wanted them to feel that way."

— Rod Dedeaux
Seven-time NCAA Division I national champion,
University of Southern California

In strength and conditioning, the SAID principle stands for Specific Adaptations to Imposed Demands. This means the body will adapt to the specific stress imposed upon it. If the body is continually called upon to perform a certain movement, doing push-ups, for example, it will adapt and increase its ability to do push-ups—but not sit-ups, pull-ups, or back flips.

In baseball, the SAID principle can be applied by mimicking the actions on the field in movement and velocity. That means doing strengthening exercises that have similar movements (i.e., rotational) and velocity (i.e., explosive). Performing other exercises is beneficial, but exercises that closely simulate the actions on the field will have the most transferability from the weight room to the diamond.

It also means practicing in a similar manner, closely mimicking games, in actions and intensity, in order for the skills to transfer most effectively to the games. One of the most important ways of doing this is to create an atmosphere of intensity and pressure in practice. Practicing under pressure forces players to focus, to use adversity, and learn to handle everything that may come their way.

Mental Mistakes Are the #1 Enemy of a Champion

Baseball lends itself to a slow, leisurely pace at times, and this can be a dangerous thing for those aspiring to win a championship. If idleness finds its way into practice, this lack of intensity will contribute to mental mistakes as much as any other factor. Players who simply go through the motions in practice will quickly find that the game is a different story.

Typically, some event occurs in a game that the players could not have prepared for, and that in itself contributes to uncertainty and mental mistakes. For example, a hitter may unexpectedly face a right-handed sidearm pitcher who throws 90 mph with a nasty slider that the other team picked up the night before. This unexpected event could turn great hitters into mediocre ones.

The ability to excel at unexpected events in a game or other pressure situations comes from that moment-to-moment intensity achieved in practice, in addition to seeing it in a game. Only when a player continually works on controlling his brain during intense situations can he really be ready to play to his full potential when that situation comes up in a game.

One way to reduce mental mistakes and inspire intense focus is to find ways to stimulate a competitive spirit on and off the field. By promoting competition among the team, engaging them with each other, and ranking them in some fashion, players will compel each other to compete. When players are constantly competing, constantly working to better themselves in pressure situations, they can adapt and learn to apply their skills in high-pressure, high-adversity conditions. These conditions create an energy on the team and in the clubhouse of competition, of always seeking to better themselves and each other.

The Competitive Cauldron

Having that energy, that competitive fire in the clubhouse, is only beneficial if it helps on the field. The top coaches are able to stoke the fires of each player in the clubhouse so they compete with each other, on and off the field. This creates energy 24 hours a day among players who are continually seeking excellence and seeking to improve.

Anson Dorrance, head coach of the University of North Carolina women's soccer team, and 17-time (yes, seventeen) national champion, says his practices are so intense he calls it a competitive cauldron.[1] He keeps statistics on anything he can in practice to rank the players, to make them compete.

Jerry Kindall did the same thing at Arizona, creating a "pressure" atmosphere in practice over and over again: "We create a lot of competition in practice. I put a clock on them, get something done in a certain amount of time so they have to do it quickly and properly. We have a lot of scrimmages; we have a lot of competition; we keep charts so they see where they're ranking. So, when they get into a game, it's not foreign to them to be in a competitive, challenging situation—we do it in practice. But, it's also a function of experience. The more times you're in that pressure-packed, stressful, focused situation, and if you have the skill, if you're doing things fundamentally correct, then you're going to succeed more often. That's the value of experience. So we create competition for them as often as we can."

Kindall's players were motivated each day because they were continually challenged to compete. They knew Kindall had a clear plan, expected high energy, and demanded constant competition. For this, Kindall won championships.

Andy Lopez's practices are built around aggressiveness and competition. He explains: "It's an aggressive approach—I want to be the aggressor; I want to be the attacker. I always tell my athletes, 'You would never get on your knees and beg your opponents for a victory, so why on earth would you do that mentally? Why would you allow yourself to mentally beg for a victory? Don't beg. Attack, attack, attack!' If you're successful, great; if you're not, keep attacking. We're going to try to put pressure on the defense. Offensively we'll bunt, run, hit-and-run, slash-and-run; we're going to let the big guys swing it, but we're going to try to attack you offensively. The foundation of everything I do is to be the aggressor."

Lopez integrates that philosophy in his everyday approach and in his practices. He teaches aggression and does it in a hands-on manner. He'll dive into a bag if he has to, slide into a base; whatever it takes to show the players how it's done. "We talk about our aggressive philosophy often. When I see something that is timid, I stop practice and point it out right on the spot. If [a player is] timid or unsure of himself, he's going to have to become sure of himself in our program. I think it's a growth process. Most of us are nervous or unsure, but we, as human beings, have to get to that stage where we are sure of ourselves; we've worked hard enough, we've paid attention to details. I speak about it all the time. When I see a timid action, whether it's a guy covering a bunt defense or a guy in a first and third offense, if he's not aggressive in his first couple steps… I'll stop practice and point it out, and say, 'That's not going to work in this environment. That uncertainty is not going to work in this environment.' So you've got to make a decision: either you're going to become very certain about what we're asking you to do, and you're going to work extra to get that technique so that you can just react instead of think, or you're just not going to make it here. We're not going to change. We're people who pay attention to detail, we're aggressive, we work hard, and we know all the concepts in our plan, and we execute them in an aggressive manner. We speak about it all the time, all the time."

Aggression in baseball comes down to the fact that baseball is an explosive, aggressive game. The best pitchers go 'right at' the hitters. The best hitters jump all over the inside fastball instead of shying away from it.

One way to simulate the intensity of a game is try to mimic the heart rate a player will get to in a game. That is what Lopez does: "Our practices are very competitive. Our baserunning is very competitive—it's catcher versus pitcher versus hitter. Every day for

10 minutes, it's live baserunning. Pitcher's trying to pick off base runners, base runners trying to steal second base, catcher's trying to throw base runners out, it's very competitive; it's game like. Most [coaches] run practices with their players' heart rates at about 40 or 50 beats per minute; I want our players at about 110 or 120 beats per minute. Because in a game setting their heart rate is not going to be 40 or 50, it's going to be 120, 130, 150, especially in the ninth inning. So, my job is to provide an intense, competitive environment where their heart rates are up, about 120. And now, in a game setting, they're used to it. It doesn't jump up and down. They here me say all the time, 'You're giving me practice speed, I want game speed.'

Lopez does everything he can in practice to get his players to game speed, to a game mindset, and to make the demands of the practice the same as a game. He puts the pressure on his players in practice. He wants his players to learn how to deal with pressure, to deal with the chaos, and to have the courage to face it, to be mentally tough. The following story shows the lengths Lopez will go to get that for his players.

Lopez: "To develop courage, I put them in as tough a situation as I can in practice. I'm a yeller and screamer. Not abusive, but for effect. I really get on some guys. I try as hard as I can some days to distract two or three individuals. I'm on them for everything—everything. I'm watching every move they make. When they mess up, I'm on them. I once had a player who I didn't think was going very hard. I followed him for five innings everywhere he went. If he got to first base, I left the dugout and stood right behind him at first base. If it was a fly ball and he was running to third, I was right there running with him. When he went to play shortstop, I'd jog right behind him and stand right behind him...in his ear the whole time for five innings. And it wasn't hugs and kisses—I was on him. I thought he was a dog and I told him. I said, 'Why do you want to play this way? You want me to do this to you every day? Because you know what? That's what I'm going to do. I'm going to stay on you until you decide to leave this program or become a man, and play like a man.' In about the fifth inning, he walked and got to first base so I ran out to first base. I started getting on him, and he turned and looked me in the eye and said, 'I've had enough.' I said 'good' and I jogged off the field. He became an All-American and we're still friends to this day."

Lopez made his point. And that's one of the reasons why he wins. His players know what it takes to win a championship. They know the intensity they need to have, the courage they need to have—he's absolutely clear about this.

Highly Structured Practices

When players are clear on what it takes to succeed, when they've got a vision, when they've got a plan, then the next step is to be highly organized with that vision and plan. Part of having a game-speed practice is having it clearly and efficiently laid out. It means having a well thought-out practice plan.

Ron Polk prepares that type of practice plan: "Our practices are highly structured, highly organized, highly disciplined, on a time schedule. I think that kids who come into our program who've never been involved in that enjoy it very much. Because they like to have structure, they like to have discipline, as long as it's fair, as long as it's concise and they know exactly what they can and cannot do."

In college baseball, there is a long wait from fall ball to opening day in the spring and some players get stagnant and lethargic. Ron Polk also puts the pressure on all year to avoid that: "In the fall program, we have player/coach evaluations where the kids evaluate each player on the ball club. We have various types of scrimmage games, we keep statistics. Anything we can do to keep them focused on 'Hey, this is a competitive situation because this is a competitive conference.'"

Championship teams don't take a winter break from competing against themselves—there's no letup from seeking improvement and excellence. There are always ways of competing, and the top teams find ways to do it. Controlling the energy in the clubhouse and directing it towards players competing with their teammates is important, as well as using it to compete with themselves.

The Practices Become the Games

Intense, game-like practice situations are so important that they may become equally as or more important than the actual games. Since (amateur) teams generally practice twice as much as they play, practice is where most of the improvement takes place.

The practice intensity of championship teams can make the games relatively easy. In essence, practices become the games, and the games become the practices. Pat Murphy explains how he prepares his players for high-pressure situations: "I think if you drill them and drill them, and make them work, and prepare them. Practices are difficult such that the game becomes like second nature. And then, you never get on them when they do not succeed results-wise, you keep emphasizing performance, performance."

If practices weigh heavier than games, and the pressure is on, then the games can be, ironically, like going through the motions (of a practice). In fact, the games ideally have less pressure than practice. The games become routine, whereas the practices are very difficult.

Gary Adams provides an intense atmosphere in practice and a loose one during games: "In practice, I'll jump all over [the players]. But in the games, I try not to put too much pressure on them. They have enough pressure anyway from their mom and dad and girlfriends that come to the game and all that. So, as a coach, I try to take off that pressure. I tell them, 'We prepared for this game; there's not going to be any surprises.

That team over there, we told you about them. There's no Babe Ruth over there; he's dead. Don't worry about pitching to anybody in their lineup.' I'm a pretty loose coach. My players know that if they make a mistake on the field in a game, I'm not going to jump on them. But in practice, I'm all over them."

To create such intensity that the practices become the games, there has to be structure, competition, and high intensity. Jerry Kindall posted his practice plan so players could see and prepare for the upcoming practice schedule. Ed Cheff's practices are so intense that the games become an average day.

Cheff explains how he gets his players to focus so well in games: "We structure the practices as high tempo, high intensity, so when we're on the field, there's not a lot of standing around. BP (batting practice) is really structured—there's three outfielders (one at each position), three base runners (one at each base) busting their butt; there's no pitchers BS-ing. You can't play structured, high-tempo, with good focus, unless everything you do is like that. In our practices, we really turn it up, turn the reality of the drills up, make it game-like, make it competitive. Then, the way we play becomes a by-product of that.

"A lot of coaches have drills that are BS, then all of the sudden they want this high-structured, bust-your-butt game mentality, and they can't figure out why their guys can't buy into that. It's because that's not how they are everyday. You play according to what you do the two or three days in practice or what you do all winter.

"Everything you do, the whole package, has to be structured and highly motivated. If I want to have low-key things then we just do it with three or four kids; it's a different kind of practice. If you're having trouble drag bunting, I'll take you and three other guys and just go out together, have fun, and screw around a little bit. You can do a little push [bunt], a little drag and I'll throw to you; it's a whole different atmosphere. It's kind of laid-back, but we're getting something done.

"But when we're in a team structure, you can't focus in on just one or two guys. I want the whole team working hard; I want everyone busting their butt, and there are times when we can have a laid-back type thing in a different setting.

"With more players, you have to be really structured, and you've got to be creative and get guys bouncing around; you don't want anyone standing around. So, you either want to be working on your hitting, your base running, or your defense—getting better. You don't want to have a practice structure that allows a guy to get bored.

"If you're a center fielder in BP, [we want you] catching everything that's hit out there, making great play after great play; all three outfielders busting their butt, seeing who can make the greatest catch. [I'll say,] 'Which one of you three guys is going to make the catch of the day today in BP?' Then, they're competing against each other.

So, you make it always a competitive thing. If you're on the bases during BP, you're busting your butt reading balls in the dirt, reading line drives, doing your thing, you're getting yourself better, then you're in to hit. BP is really structured; there's a lot going on, it's not just a coach throwing BP to one guy while a bunch of pitchers are hanging around the outfield BS-ing...

Another way to induce intensity and encourage competition in practice is to single out players who make great plays. Players like acknowledgment and status, and being held in high esteem by the coach in front of the other players is one way to give them that. Cheff acknowledges that effort: "I yell it out, 'Hey, that's the play of the day so far.' Then, the other guy's going to try to belly out. They're looking for that—who can make the most great plays. 'Hey, Smith great play'; well, Smith's going, 'Hey, Johnson how many great plays you got today?' 'I only have one'. Then, Johnson gets another one. Now, this is good for the kids. I made three great plays today. So when BP's done, you get everyone together and total it up; who had some great plays, what was the greatest play you saw today?

Practical Application

In order to get players to progress beyond cognitive understanding to practical application, they have to be tested. They may know what to do, and how to do it, but can they actually do it when the pressure's on? That's the key—taking the coaching, the knowledge, and the skills, and making them work during the game.

Cheff likes to simulate the last three innings—the pressure innings of the game: "We have a drill where we try to create game situations off a fungo [bat] with live runners. The players take the knowledge, and they have to put it in the lab [on the field], and the lab has to mirror a game situation. It has to be live. I'm not going to measure your application of the knowledge in a non-pressure situation—it doesn't mean anything."

Players can practice a drill over and over and over, but they also need the pressure that may accompany the execution of their skills during a game; without it, their application of the skill can never be really trusted in a game. Cheff uses pitchers as an example: "As soon as pitchers start doing bunt defense drills trying to get lead runners, after three [times], nobody's going to make a mistake. They're all good now. But all of a sudden in the seventh inning, bang—we're there, and you have to do it; some guys have a hard time making a practical application of the knowledge.

"You have to create those types of practice situations all the time, where it's not just drill after drill after drill. It's game situation-type things, and bang-bang, you're orchestrating with a fungo one play after another after another, and you're just going from a double relay to a bunt rotation and its bang-bang-bang. You're creating live game situations."

"You can't just do it in a drill. The first time we do it in a drill we might screw it up, then we do it 10 times and we get it right, but that doesn't mean three days from now we will. Because I don't know if they have practical application yet; I know they understand the concept, but I don't know if they can apply it yet. So, I have to keep testing to see if they can apply it."

Getting players to be able to apply their skills when needed means creating competitive situations where they fail. They need to learn how to deal with failure and to bounce back from it. That's one of the biggest challenges in baseball as well as in all of athletics (and life).

Kindall explains: "There's going to be failure in practice for Arizona baseball players. There's going to be guys who rank above them. There's going to be a challenge to get there, to the top rung in practice as well as in the game. The more times you put a player in competitive situations and watch him carefully and chart him, and lovingly and understandably and supportably watch him in competition…you'll see that some guys rise to the top, some guys sink below that, and that's your starting lineup."

Skip Bertman said, "Get comfortable with failure because you can't succeed without risk and risk brings failure." Bertman's teams got so comfortable with failure that they won five national championships in 10 years. They failed over and over again, and that's why they succeeded.

With Pressure Comes Adversity and Failure

To be successful, Bertman's teams had to take risks, and they had to fail. He continually put his teams in situations where they could fail. He knew that success, true success, comes after failure. Great accomplishments are only great because they have failure attached to them.

Pat Murphy's teams sought out that kind of adversity starting with a tough schedule; a schedule where they had to face challenges and deal with adversity. He explains: "I always like to play a tough schedule. I'm not worrying about the gaudy record, just being there at the end. I like to make sure that everybody is playing aggressively. You cannot coast uphill."

For Murphy and other top coaches, the big goal is not to win every game *during* the season, it's to win the last game of the season (e.g., the championship). As long as the team wins enough games to make the playoffs, winning more than that is not essential.

What's more important than winning the "non-essential" games is improving as a team, and coming through in pressure situations. If the team has already clinched a playoff spot, that might be a good time to use the last player on the bench in a pressure situation to prepare him for a similar situation in the playoffs.

When you risk playing a tough schedule like Murphy does, therein lies possible failure, possible down times. But that is where the championship mentality comes into play: rebounding from hard times, refusing to internalize failures, and working harder to improve.

Pat Murphy explains the importance of dealing with adversity: "The thing that I look for most in players is how they handle adversity. You have to handle that with character and integrity, for sure. How are you going to compete after you get knocked on your butt?"

Pressure and Adversity Brings Aggression

When players do get knocked down, the good ones become aggressive. Aggression is an important element that comes with induced pressure. The pressure brings adversity, and adversity brings aggression in top players. They know they have to step up in the face of adversity, whatever that may be (an individual or a situation).

During a game or season, there will be instances when players will need to take out the second baseman trying to turn the double play. A situation may dictate needing to take out the catcher on a close play at the plate. Or, there might be a close play along the fence, and he may have to slide into the fence to catch the ball. As Andy Lopez knows, aggression is a very important part of winning baseball.

Aggression can manifest itself in many ways, but, importantly, in baseball it is a demeanor that gets players to jump up when they're knocked down, to overcome adversity, and to face their fears. Aggression keeps players from sinking into mediocrity. Unless prompted otherwise, players can easily move toward being comfortable and having a lackadaisical attitude.

Cheff's constant pressure on his players makes sure they never get too comfortable: "Sometimes, even if a guy does everything right for you, you have to get on him, just to get on him. It may be hard to find a fault, but then pretty soon nobody hears him getting chewed out. So, he's almost not one of the guys. So, you have to keep that consistency. Don't jump on some poor freshman and vent your rage on him, while you got some stud who you treat differently. I'll never treat a star player differently than an average guy. In fact, I'm going to be a little more critical of him."

Principle #7
Practice Under Pressure

A baseball game may take two and a half hours to play, but winning or losing can come down to what happens in the two or three big pressure situations that occur. Or as San Francisco Giants' general manager Brian Sabean simplified it: "Baseball comes down to what your hitters do with men on base and what your pitcher does with men on base." What happens during those crucial moments when the pressure is on, determines the outcomes of most games.

It is during those instances that a player needs to be completely focused, and in the moment. His nervous system should be fully alert while having an inner calm—ready for any possible situation. Achieving the goal of winning the pitch in the crucial situations is enhanced by repeatedly experiencing those situations. Whether in practice or a game, having been through pressure situations enables players to win the crucial pitches.

Basically, it comes down to a mental game, one where pressure is the name of the game. To succeed in those pressure moments, players need to be prepared for them, mentally and physically. It's one thing to perform under non-confrontational conditions, but it's another thing entirely to do so in the midst of intense competition, when the game's on the line and the crowd is going crazy. Those are the times when it really counts, and those are the situations where championship teams excel.

CHAPTER 8

Excel in the Exclusive Moment

"We talk about the opportunity of what I call the 'exclusive moment' in every ball game. Every one of you will have an opportunity, or multiple opportunities, to be that person in that exclusive moment when the game is on the line. I expect each one of you to aspire for that, to long for that opportunity, and I believe that each one of you can come through in that opportunity."

— Carroll Land, Ph.D.
Point Loma Nazarene University

Every game has a defining moment, a time where the spectators are on the edges of their seats, there's electricity in the air, and the game is on the line. In most sports, the last two minutes of the game is when the chaos is at its peak. In baseball, the big moment can come with the bases loaded in the bottom of the ninth, or the bottom of the first. Winning teams execute in those crucial moments.

Winning teams are much more confident that they will succeed than other teams are because they've developed a deep-seated belief in themselves. They've visualized the moment over and over in their minds, and they've seen it on video. They recognize what to do when these situations come about, and they know how to handle the pressure.

Champions won't execute every time; in fact, sometimes they'll choke. That doesn't scare them, because they accept it as part of the game. They're not even afraid of being afraid, because they welcome fear as a force they can use. They've been in scary situations before and know they're going to win that moment more often than not, and when they don't, they learn from it and move to the next moment.

Champions learn to control their physical and mental responses to these pressure situations and get into their ideal performance state, "the zone." They have rituals that help with this such as taking deep breaths, talking to one's self, and performing physical routines. When the pressure's on they learn to control their adrenaline and execute, at times flawlessly, as if they're designed for that moment. They are.

The Facts About Pressure

Webster's dictionary defines pressure as *a compelling influence or constraining force*. Champions are able to use pressure in the former sense of the word rather than the latter. When used as a "compelling influence," it can be a positive energy that compels players to succeed in the exclusive moment. When players feel the "constraining force," it impedes any skill the player may have.

Pressure comes from how players view a situation, not the situation itself. James Loehr explains that "pressure is when you're afraid of the possible negative consequences of missing a shot, or striking out in the ninth. If you know you're going to get that base hit, there's no pressure. If you think, 'What if I fail?' then you're in trouble."[1]

It takes mental toughness and preparation to deal with pressure. The ability to execute under pressure comes from visualizing a situation before it happens, repeatedly. This means physically and mentally experiencing the pressure situations and finally, looking forward to these situations—anticipating that exclusive moment and being ready for the mind games that will inevitably come.

Bob Todd explains pressure: "If you're a professional bowler and you start bowling a game...you start off frame one, strike, frame two, strike, three and all of the sudden you come to the last frame and you've got a perfect game going. Is there any more pressure on you to roll that last ball for a strike for a perfect game than there was in frame three? No. If you are doing everything you possibly can to be the best that you can be, then frame three to you mentally is no different than frame 10, the last ball you roll. You are going to do anything you can to be the best you can be. There's no difference. So pressure is internally produced. Pressure is not external, it's internal."

Pressure is not only internal, but it is unique to each person. In the words of philosopher Deepak Chopra: "Reality is what *you* think it is." Everyone has a different paradigm for viewing the world; each person creates his or her own reality and pressure is no different—it's created by the individual.

The problem with pressure is that the athlete's focus narrows and cues are missed which are necessary to perform well. Instead of focusing on the situation, the player starts noticing internal things such as muscle tension, an accelerating heart rate, etc. Then, if he starts thinking about the possible negative end result, that creates more pressure.

Ancient samurai Miyamoto Musashi says that fear, anxiety, or nervous anticipation, comes with living in the past or future. Live in the moment. Realize that the external environment cannot cause these feelings unless the person allows it. "When your mind 'stops' to question or decide or judge—when you are concentrating on that, you lose track of what is still going on," Musashi says.[2]

During competition, emotions run high and the athlete who can control his frustration, doubt, and negative thoughts will have the edge. Players who are able to control their thoughts are able to manage pressure well. They've become disciplined thinkers and have learned to block out negative thoughts, not eliminate them (they will always be near) but stop them when they come.

Welcome the Pressure

Champions believe they are designed for defining moments, that all their lives have been preparation for those moments. Therefore, they seek them out, they welcome the pressure. After all, that's one of the things champions do best, perform under pressure.

These top performers view pressure and adversity as challenges, not threats. They're not afraid they'll "choke"—they know they will, sooner or later. Every superstar hitter has struck out with the game on the line. That's how they became superstars— they put themselves in situations so many times and learned something each time. Michael Jordan, perhaps the greatest basketball player ever, has missed countless do-or-die shots in the waning seconds of a game. Legendary slugger Babe Ruth held the home run record *and* the strikeout record, but he craved those pressure situations; he was the hero and the goat. He was challenged by those situations and took the risk.

The words of Theodore Roosevelt reverberate with wisdom regarding those risks: "Far better it is to dare mighty things, to win glorious triumphs, even though checkered by failure, than to rank with those poor spirits who neither enjoy much nor suffer much because they live in the gray twilight that knows neither victory nor defeat." Roosevelt may have been thinking of another U.S. president, Abraham Lincoln, when he uttered those words. Lincoln failed again and again, personally and professionally, before becoming president. Both took risks, both knew what it was like to fail, and, consequently, they achieved greatness.

The best competitors look forward to "glorious triumphs checkered with failure." Triumph and failure go hand in hand, because success, as often noted, is on the far side of failure. The best, most talented players and coaches crave competition so much that they would rather lose than not have tried at all.

A key ingredient in those who are successful is that they want to be in the heat, they're not afraid to fail. For Terry Francona, the pressure situations are the reason he enjoys managing, and it's why he played: "My favorite thing is in the close games, like in the eighth and ninth inning, when it's a one-run game, it's kind of gut-wrenching, that's about as close to being a player as you can get. You're sitting in the dugout, you're nervous, you're trying to do the right thing, and it's fun. Even when you lose, I think you'd almost rather have that feeling of just devastation rather than having no feeling at all," Francona explains.

Three-time Canadian wrestling champion and 2002 Commonwealth Games gold medalist Nick Ugoalah credits much of his success to the adversity he's had in his life. He learned how to handle it, and use it to his advantage. He does the same thing with pressure. "Pressure becomes a part of me that I welcome," he says, "it's no longer the enemy." Ugoalah takes the energy that comes with pressure, that makes the heart race, and channels it toward his opponent. He embraces those big moments.

Ed Cheff looks for guys who have dreamed about being champions in pressure moments since childhood: "You can't be the hero unless you're in the heat. Do you want to be there or not? Why are you playing? You play because you want it on the line. If there's a runner on second and you're up, a lot of guys say, 'Shoot I hope he walks me.'

"You hope you pick out the right guys who are on the field for you. Guys dream about that stuff. You've dreamed about seeing yourself drive in the winning run since you were six years old. Kids fantasize about those things, and they see it. You have to really believe that it's going to be true someday. I mean you dreamed about it forever, now here it is. If you didn't dream about it, you shouldn't be playing," Cheff explains.

Preparation Lessens Pressure

To get from the dreaming stage to excelling under pressure takes intensive practice, physically and mentally. Players who regularly visualize the sweet success of coming through in the clutch and prepare for it physically are those who win. It doesn't happen without lots of intense preparation.

Tom House describes the importance of preparation: "My philosophy is that the best player does not always win, the best prepared player wins. With that in mind, if you can convince a kid that he is the best prepared he can be, then he will go into competition much more confident about his ability to succeed.

"You can't go from preparation to success. You have to have a system of cognitive support that will allow the player to handle the ups and downs of competition without coming apart. That only comes with preparation."

So it's not just preparation, but preparing for the exclusive moments and all the accompanying pressure. When players do that, they have confidence that facilitates coming through in those situations.

Art Howe, manager of the 2000 and 2002 American League West champion Oakland A's, is a big believer that preparation enables players to deal with pressure: "If you're on edge, nervous or unprepared, which is a good reason to be nervous, you don't get it done. You've got to be mentally tough. Being physically prepared takes the pressure off mentally. If you've done everything you can to prepare for this game, now it's just a matter of executing."

Jim Leyland discusses pressure in a similar manner as Howe: "I think first of all it's something you continue to work at. Number two, you explain that there's good pressure and bad pressure. Good pressure is when you're prepared. Good pressure is when the situation comes up and you're prepared for it. It's still pressure but it's good pressure. Bad pressure is when you haven't prepared and all of the sudden the situation comes up and now you're lost because you haven't prepared for it. So there's two types of pressure. I try to get my players in a position where they feel the good pressure."

Don't downplay the situation

Instead of preparing for and feeling the good (compelling) pressure, a lot of coaches downplay a situation that is absolutely huge. If they lose they have a built-in excuse, like the school kid who loses a game of four square: "I wasn't really trying," he may say.

Coaches (and players) often do the same thing. They enter a playoff game, or a crucial situation and act like it's not as big as it is. The problem is that the players know when it's the biggest game of the year. Avoiding the topic or walking on eggshells may put more pressure on them.

What helps is to talk about *the game* and the final at-bat of the big game on the first day of practice. Then daily between then and when it actually occurs, discuss, dream, and visualize winning the big moment in the big game. It's impossible to practice it a hundred times and prepare a hundred times without it getting into the players' subconscious.

If it's not discussed and prepared for, players will stress about it subconsciously throughout the year. Then when the big game arrives it becomes one huge pressure situation. Not preparing for the exclusive moment(s) in a game is preparing to lose.

The important thing is not to try to reduce the pressure by ignoring it, or downplaying it, but by being prepared mentally and physically. Start on the first day of the season getting the players excited about being in that pressure situation, seeing themselves succeeding. Then put them in that pressure situation with intense practice mentally and physically, starting from the opening practice.

Once it's game day the focus is strictly on competing—just like practice. Nothing different whatsoever, just competing, forgetting about results. There are so many variables in baseball that can't be controlled, just focus on what can be controlled. It's not downplaying or uplaying anything. It's playing hard all the time.

Ed Cheff wins national championships because he expects to win the exclusive moments in each game, especially big games. He doesn't undersell the big game. The big game is the big game.

"A lot of coaches say that, well we're going to the national championship but it's not important if we win. They sell themselves that if it's not important, than they wont feel bad if they lose. Some players are like that; you get into pressure games, and some guys don't want to make it really, really important because they don't want to hurt if they lose it. So they'd rather find a way to rationalize it out and say 'well this is not really important, this is not a matter of life and death, if we win ok'; they try to reduce stress that way," Cheff says.

Focus on the game and competition, not the result

Instead of downplaying the big game, focus on the details of the game, not the consequences. Teams get so caught up in winning and losing that they lose track of the game. They listen to the media and armchair QB's who over-dramatize the results and forget the process, and the joy of competing. It's easy to forget it's about playing the game, not the accolades.

One of the great things about playing the game is the competition. Whether it's playing a game of pick-up basketball or being up to bat in a crucial situation, the competition is what makes athletics exciting. Like Francona said, the things that come with competition: excitement, nervousness, pressure—that's the good stuff. The great part is the journey not the destination.

Focus on the destination during visualization and the journey during the event. For most star athletes, dreaming about succeeding under pressure comes natural. It's so natural in fact that they don't even realize they've been preparing for the big game since they were old enough to play. Focusing on the journey becomes much harder as players get older, as they've been bombarded by the media and armchair QB's for so many years they begin to feel their pressure and forget how much they love the game.

Ed Cheff puts it into perspective for his players: "I think if you can get them to reduce stress by saying, hey this is great, win or lose this is going to be a war today, lets just enjoy the experience. Let's enjoy the game, not worry about the result, enjoy the competitiveness, and try to get guys to think. The key is to enjoy the game, enjoy the competition. Piss on the result."

At Point Loma Nazarene, Carroll Land pushes the same concept to his players: "If you return to those fundys (fundamental drills) that we work on every day and you isolate the consequence from the act, and just dwell on the act, then the consequence will turn out in your favor more often than not. We try to divorce the result. We do not talk much about the result. We talk about the process."

When a player can focus solely on the act and enjoy it, in the heat of the moment, then he can excel. Loehr says hockey legend Wayne Gretzky credited much of his success to his ability to maintain a moment-to-moment focus during play and have fun as he performs.[3] That's an important element, having fun. When a player can enjoy the game during the heat of the moment then he can achieve peak performance. He's got to be able to step back amidst the chaos, smile, and think "This is right where I want to be." That's what Gretzky did.

Get the players to believe in themselves

The best players have dreamed about being stars since they were kids, and they continually dream about it—it never stops. They want to be the guy, the man, who excels in the exclusive moment. They've got the ability, the mental picture, and they believe in themselves.

With a lot of self confidence they get the most out of their ability, especially when it counts. To get that confidence they need to have had some success, overcome some adversity, and have a coach who believes in them. When they develop that unwavering belief, then the exclusive moments become enjoyable too.

Davey Johnson knows his players can't perform their best unless they have that resolute belief in their ability. He explains: "My biggest role is to get the players to believe in themselves and to believe in myself. No question."

Johnson's first year managing was in double A with the Mets in Jackson, Mississippi. He molded a group of players who were not picked to win many games into a championship team. He got them believing in themselves. He explains: "They thought we had the fewest prospects in the whole organization but we didn't, we had a bunch of gamers, and we ended up winning the Texas league championship."

They didn't win because they were the most talented, they won because they had players who Davey had instilled a strong belief that they could come through in the clutch: "You have to realize from a manager's standpoint, even though you know this guy will never get out of double A, you have to treat him just like he was the number one prospect. You have to have just as much confidence in him, and boost his confidence. They all think they're going to play in the big leagues. It's very important you get that feeling to everybody," Johnson explains.

"I found one thing that's a truism, if I didn't think a guy could play, he couldn't. So if I expected them all to do it, I had to act like they all could do it. I had to convince them that I believed in them. Not just talking it, not lip service, but by giving them the opportunity. I could say you're the greatest hitter I ever saw in the world, you're wonderful, but if I pinch-hit for you in the third inning, you say I don't trust this SOB worth anything. Or, if I say you're a good fielder and I put in somebody on defense for you, or if you know you have a problem with defense and I leave you out there and let you play, I'm showing confidence in you. Pretty soon you're going to have confidence in yourself, and your going to get better, if you have the heart. If you work at it, you're going to get it done, because I believe in you, and you'll believe in yourself. I think its just part of being successful, giving a guy the opportunity to be successful."

Giving players the opportunity to succeed or fail is a tangible thing where the player can see the coach believes in him. That's just as important as telling him how good he is; they go together.

Terry Collins elevates his players' play in pressure situations by communicating with them, showing confidence in them: "I think it's a matter of communication; you have to let them know that they're good, and that pressure's all part of it. That's why they're here, because they were the best available; [I tell them to] walk up there because they can get the job done. I tell guys there's not a situation that's gone by that I don't put a player in where I think he's got a chance to be the most successful. Therefore I have confidence in him, and if they know you have confidence in them their confidence in themselves gets better. Then they deal with pressure better. The minute they think that someone's against them or you don't have confidence in them, then you lose them. There's a lot of times you see a guy give up a hit in the ninth inning; the worst thing that can happen is to turn around and walk away from him. You're mad because he gave up the hit, even if he loses the game [I'll tell him] 'shoot you're going back out there tomorrow because you're my guy.' I think if you can instill that confidence in your players, it'll help them be better."

Instilling confidence in players is important in helping them succeed in pressure situations. Talking to them, knowing what makes them tick as individuals, showing genuine care, and believing in them—it all adds up to a more confident player, one who will play to his potential more often, and will come through in the clutch. Recruiting players with mental toughness along with physical ability is a common theme among championship coaches, and instilling an unyielding sense of confidence in each player.

Self confidence is so critical in athletic competition that legendary football coach John Robinson had this to say about it: "I never criticize a player until they are first convinced of my unconditional confidence in their abilities."

Get in the zone

What players are continually striving for, is to get into the state of mind where they can use their self-confidence, preparation, and skill to the utmost. Those things often go out in the window in pressure situations because of the mental daggers that cut down the weak-minded. The self-doubt and fear of failure mount up with the screaming crowd and the chaos. Players need to be able to overcome those limiting thoughts and noises, and get into a zone where they play their best—where they have a heightened awareness.

In this zone time slows down and everything flows. Athletes describe their performance almost as if they were outside their body watching it happen; a surreal feeling where they know how the end of the script will pan out, where nothing matters but the present moment. The heart rate slows down, as do the brain waves, which is a good thing. Slow waves equals quick reactions.[4] This kind of focus, this supreme concentration, intensity, and determination is what all athletes aspire to but few can summon very often. The ones that do are called superstars.

Dusty Baker talks about being in the zone in the pressure situations: "When you get to that situation you have to continue to breathe [instead of] hyperventilate. You have to get to the point where even though your heart is pumping fast and has that burning desire to succeed, your mind remains cool in order to control your heart. Because if not you get caught up in the tempo of the game and caught up with the fans. And last but not least you have to concentrate and relax to the point where your mind separates from your body. Imagine a puppeteer above the stadium controlling you down there versus you down there being a puppet looking up; it's massive when you look up there. You have to get to the point where you concentrate so much that time almost sort of stops, everything slows down."

This kind of concentration and focus enables athletes to surmount any magnitude of pressure. Pitchers get the strikeout with the bases loaded in the bottom of the ninth; hitters get game-winning hits. Getting into this zone defies pressure.

Visualize the zone experience

Visualizing those pressure situations help players get into the zone. Getting in the zone takes practice visualizing the pressure situations and executing. If a player can create pressure situations in his mind day after day, simulating himself coming through in the clutch, his mind remembers it as if it happened.

Psychologists call this mental imagery with "induced affect." Having the player imagine stressful situations and generating high levels of emotional arousal, then using coping skills to "turn off" the emotional arousal. The key is utilizing all the senses to create a vivid picture, as discussed in chapter three.

It's also important to see and feel the end results. Hitters should see the first base coach giving them a high-five, their teammates mobbing them after the game-winning hit, the interview after the game, all that.

The goal with visualizing being in the zone and excelling in the exclusive moments is to invoke a nervous system response. The nervous system responds when it feels pain, fear, or other emotions. For example when people think about the thing in life they are most scared of, be it jumping out of a plane, speaking to a large group, or falling into a pit full of vipers, if they think about it vividly, their nervous system will start sending messages to the body to begin firing adrenaline. Their palms become sweaty, their heart rate accelerates, and they may even find it hard to breathe. So they've done nothing but imagine it yet their body reacted with a physical response as if it was real.

That's the key to visualizing being in the zone. Imagine the most intense, pressure-packed confrontation using all the senses, get the nervous system to start firing the adrenaline, then have the player see himself executing under pressure and the subsequent high fives, the cheering, etc.

Learning to breathe deeply is a big part of visualization and arousal control.[5] It helps the athlete get in the right mental state, sort of a meditative consciousness. This deep breathing is then replicated on the field to slow the heart rate in "pressure" situations.

An excellent way to get in the zone while visualizing is to sit tall on the floor and take ten slow, deep breaths, counting in for four, holding it for four, then exhaling for four. During this time block all thoughts out and clear the mind. Then when the heart rate is decelerated, the visualizing begins.

The player starts by visualizing the atmosphere and then inserting himself into the tense situation. It helps if it's a really pressure packed situation and everything is chaos—the crowd screaming and stomping, the guys on the bench with their rally hats on, etc.

Author Stephen Covey describes helping his son use visualization, relaxation, and deep breathing with the pressure situations he faced in football. As the quarterback he would visualize himself right in the heat of the toughest situations imaginable. With a big blitz coming, he would audibilize (call another play at the last second) and get the first down.[6]

Psychologist Tom Hanson interviewed Hall-of-Famer Hank Aaron to see how he got into the zone. Aaron stated that his primary means of mentally preparing was visualization. Visualizing himself facing pitchers in various situations throughout the day fostered his great focus during each at-bat. His mental preparation involved:

1. From the night before and throughout the day he would visualize facing the next game's pitcher in a variety of different situations.

2. During the game he continued visualization, studying the pitcher's motion and release, looking for cues that tip off his pitches early.

3. On deck he kept his eyes on the pitcher, studying his motion and release

4. In the batter's box he focused in on the pitcher like looking down a tunnel, effectively blocking out any possible distractions.

What Aaron did was put himself in a place where mentally he pictured his desired result, and got his mind and heart rate at a place optimum to best use his considerable skills.

Videos to program the mind

Videos are an excellent way to visualize the zone experience, and get the heart and mind in peak performance mode, to facilitate excelling in the exclusive moment. Skip Bertman, one of the master motivators in the game, used videos to imprint on his players' minds past and future successes. Before their playoff game against Virginia Commonwealth (May 2001) Skip quietly explained the plan of attack; who their opponents best players were, who was hitting the ball well, a few words about the starting pitcher, etc. He read a short quote that he had printed and after a short talk, they played a video came on their big screen tv in the locker room (as they do before every game). It was about an eight-minute video showing Omaha, site of the College World Series (CWS), past successes of the current team, and past national champions winning it all.

Skip was preparing the players for pressure situations (the video showed the stadium, the crowds, the players, the fans, game footage, etc.) --planting a winning frame of mind. Now when the players get to Omaha they've seen it, they've visualized it, and they've seen their past teams winning it all. Before every game, Skip's players saw themselves and other LSU players excelling in pressure situations, in big games. This imprinted in their minds winning the exclusive moment.

Programming the mind is not something that can be done overnight. It's like trying to change an old habit, it takes time. A player's mind has had habits and patterns of thought since childhood and reprogramming those patterns of thought takes time. But it can be done. Sometimes it takes months, sometimes years, sometimes a lifetime. Here's how Andy Lopez did it.

Building a champion: How Pepperdine won the College World Series

In 1992 Pepperdine became the smallest school in the history of college baseball to win a national championship. They were the 7th seed in Omaha (out of eight). "We walked in and they didn't even know how to say our name," Lopez states. So how did they end up winning it all? Many factors; it was a process over three years. That team was his first recruiting class who were now juniors, so he had been working with many of the players for the past three years. And their number one trait? "Courage, tremendous courage," Lopez says.

Every day Lopez works on his players to be mentally tough and more courageous. For Lopez, courage is the consummate trait of a champion, and what he tries to instill in all his players. Getting them to have the courage to put themselves in do or die situations, the courage to risk failure, the courage to believe in themselves when no one else does, and the courage to never give up. His intensity and belief in his players gave them the courage to excel in the exclusive moments on the journey to and during the CWS.

"Now this [team was the culmination of] three years of working on working on courage, and be on time, and do things right, and intensity, and competitive practices; scheduling the best teams we could schedule, and going everywhere, going to Texas, going to Stanford, going to Fresno, going to Arizona. At Pepperdine you're never going to host a regional so our strategic plan for our scheduling was to go to the places we might one day be in a regional. In other words, go there, play three games, because you may just get back there. Well lo and behold, we went to Tucson in 1991 and beat Arizona two out of three there. In 1992 guess where our regional was. So it wasn't a new experience for our guys, and not only that, but they won two out of three here. So I said 'Hey fellas we've been here once, let's do it again.' So it was an accumulation of three years of work."

It took Lopez three years to create that belief, that courage.

"In '92 we went to Stanford in February and we got swept in a three game series by three walk-off home runs (game-winning home run to end the game). So those guys could've packed their bags and said, 'Wow, we've been shooting for this for three years and we just got swept in Stanford in three heartbreaks.' So that's the one characteristic: courage. About a month and a half later Stanford came to LA and we beat them soundly. And I think we won something like 36 games out of our next 38 to win the national championship.

"We were on a roll, but those guys went through some tough times. We went to play the university of San Francisco sometime in March of '92, and we win two out of three, and I thought we should have won all three games. We played real sloppy and lost the last game. Now this is the team that would go on to win the national championship in a few months. So we're at the airport in San Francisco and our guys are loosey goosey, laughing, and I was upset because I thought we just gave that last game away. We flew into LA at ten o-clock that night and I got them together and I said 'we're going to be in uniform at midnight tonight, we're going to practice. I'll see you at midnight.' We didn't have lights at Pepperdine. That was before the rules were in place, where you could do that. I can't do that now. We worked out for two hours."

Learn Internal Control Techniques

In addition to imprinting success mentally, players need to find ways to control their nervous system during games. Players need to regulate their heart rates and thought processes; they need to be monitored, just like any other aspect of the game.

Tom Trebelhorn agrees: I like to see more relaxation techniques. When they feel like they're going too fast, or things are ahead of them, they have techniques to slow themselves down and checkpoints. I work a lot on what works; some guys we can do that and that refocuses. Some guys do an eye-stretch, try to do some trigger mechanism that settles that particular player down or gets them to refocus or gets them back into the mode they have to be in."

Deep breathing, taking long, slow, deep breaths is one of the most common methods of controlling the heart rate. Many players integrate this technique into their routines, as well as during their mental practice. Dusty Baker describes superior athletes who have supreme focus and are able to block everything out while controlling their breathing: "Whether it's Michael Jordan, or Wayne Gretzky, you have to have that ability to focus and concentrate and to continue to breathe because it is so important. It's probably the thing we take for granted the most."

Self Talk and Affirmations During Competition

Although breathing is a natural process, during periods of high stress or in pressure situations, shallow breathing often results. Learning to breathe naturally in tense situations, to perform fluidly and freely, comes from mental practice.

For Jerry Stitt, former head coach at Arizona, mental preparation cannot be overstated: "We have times where we do nothing but mental work. We teach them how to do imagery. We teach them how to breathe and the different things you need to do in game situations to get rid of the stress: positive self-talk, those kinds of things."

Self-talk comprises the thoughts players have about themselves. Things like, *"Come on Jim, you're better than that."* Crash Davis in the movie *Bull Durham*, talks to himself (and the pitcher) while he is hitting: "Come on Meat", he says, "bring in that heater so I can crush it." That's Crash Davis's self-talk in the form of an affirmation.

Affirmations are statements that 'affirm' what the player would like to be his reality. For example, if he wants to be the best hitter in the league, he may have an affirmation such as, "Opposing managers are always nervous when I hit because I am the best hitter in the league." So the affirmation is always positive, always in the present tense, and should evoke some emotion or feeling. Affirmations should be based on the dream too—that hero moment. For example, "I am the RBI master and always come through in clutch situations." If a left-handed batter has been having trouble facing left-handed pitchers, he may have an affirmation such as "I crush lefties." It's simple, positive, in the present tense, and evokes some emotion.

Tom House said, "Affirmations are the only thing that I found that you can make a kid responsible for and it actually becomes a part of his process."

Affirmations are more powerful when they're written down and reviewed daily. Putting them all over the place forces them to be read. A short list of affirmations can be placed right next to the player's bed for him to read out loud when he wakes up and when he goes to sleep. Doing this every day will affix it in the player's mind and soon it will be a regular part of his thoughts; then, his self-image and, subsequently, his performance will work to match it. That's the power of affirmations.

Affirmations program the mind and acts as a supplement to a visual picture of the desired results. They are clearly written out, read repeatedly, and visualized. With this imprinted on a player's brain, the spare moments he has all day long can be used to his advantage, repeating positive affirmations.

Tom House discusses affirmations: "I like to use affirmations, they give each kid a sense of self. You have to find a way for a guy to be responsible and accountable for the work ethic, but then find a way to affirm that the work ethic is going to be a payoff when he gets competitive."

The important instance is after the doubt has arrived. After the player's thoughts say, "Wow, I'm really struggling," the player's self-talk either affirms the negative thought or denies it. Tom House describes how Nolan Ryan used self-talk: "I can remember Nolan saying, "Dang it, Nolan, that's the right pitch, but it was the wrong darn location, now turn the page..." He got over the feeling of the screw up and on to the next thought process; he was reprogrammed. So, he didn't dwell at the point in time, and he always had a positive statement about himself or the task for the next pitch."

Having Rituals

Most every professional athlete has some sort of ritual for when he's on the mound, in the on-deck circle, or in pre game—something that helps him get into the zone. A ritual is a routine of performing the same actions and thinking the same thoughts to induce a certain state of mind. It's like how a song can bring back a special time and place; that song triggers a state of mind.

Rituals can do the same thing for inducing "the zone" mindset, or as Loehr refers to it, "the ideal performance state." It is an ideal inner climate from which top performances come. It allows actions to be easy and automatic. Breathing techniques, self-talk, and visualization are all part of the rituals professionals employ, whether they're on-deck or between pitches on the mound. Rituals allow the athlete to become physically relaxed, focused, confident, and able to enjoy the competition. Taking a few long, slow deep breaths in the on-deck circle can enhance the preparation of any hitter.

Relaxation versus Fierce Determination

Playing hard externally and being relaxed internally is the goal of most top athletes, but is it the ideal combination for success? Being able to relax in pressure situations is difficult to do, and may not be the preeminent thing anyway. The desired result is achieving optimum performance in high-stress, crucial situations. How is that best achieved? It goes back to the ideal state of mind—the zone—which is different for each person.

The ideal state for some athletes can mean a more relaxed state, while for others it may mean an intense state of mind. Either way, it's getting to a place where the athlete focuses solely on the task at hand and doesn't let his mind hinder his ability to come through in the pressure situation. Seattle Mariners first baseman John Olerud is so smooth and relaxed at the plate. But is he more relaxed or more intense internally? Only he knows. And maybe he doesn't even know. Olerud does, however, know how to get into that zone, and that's all he needs to know.

Ed Cheff is an intense coach, and he demands the same thing from his players. How does he get his players to relax? "I don't want them to relax. I want them to kick their butts. I don't believe in that (relaxing). I want our hitter to get eye contact with their pitcher and say 'I'm going to kick your butt right now.' Now maybe that helps them relax. I teach them to relax by making it a one on one competition. I can relax by bearing down to kick your butt. Focus in, take the challenge."

He requires the same intensity from his pitchers. Cheff continues: "I tell my pitchers, 'Make eye contact right before you pitch. Especially if this guy's a drag bunter and he likes to do anything cute with the bat. Look him right in the eye and first pitch knock him right on his butt.' So, he won't be dinking around doing that. Never throw to hit the guy, just get him off the plate, put a little fear in him. He's not going to drag bunt now. He doesn't want any part of that drag bunt. And that helps the pitcher relax. I'm not going to think, *Man, I can't walk this guy, the guy might drag bunt on me.* I can make that guy not want to bunt with one pitch. Take a fast one under your chin, now see if you're going to stick your nose in to drag bunt. If he's a real tough kid he will, but that's my way of relaxing. That's different than what some guys say, you have to relax."

Whether being in the zone is relaxing or not, it is a state of focused aggression. It's a player using the skills he has to the utmost, and being ready to be the aggressor when the situation warrants it. Rod Delmonico also wants his players to have that intensity, that aggression: "It's an attitude. When I step into the box, I want that guy to know I'm here to do business. It's the way I carry myself, it's my body language, the way I step into the box. I've done my work. I've worked hard in the cages. I'm mentally prepared. I saw myself being successful. You ain't beating me. It's an attitude. When I step into the box, you better be excellent or you aren't going to beat me. If you can get all your hitters to do that, you're going to have success."

The relaxation/intensity scale can vary from player to player and position to position. For example, a starting pitcher's mental approach may be much different than a closer. It'd be difficult for a guy like Trevor Hoffman (Padres closer) to have the same intensity if he were a starter as he does as a closer. Walking out to a song from rock group AC/DC in the first inning might not sustain him for five innings. The point is, some coaches want their players relaxed, some want them intense. They all however, want each player to be in the zone where he's playing at his peak.

Tom House describes the ideal mental state for handling a pressure situation: "In my opinion, you can make the body relax with deep breathing but nobody relaxes in competition. That zone that people get in, I think they achieve it with either too much adrenaline or the ability to redirect the adrenaline into a point to where everything in the body is lined up. Relaxation, to me, is a nice psychological word that has very little meaning in the everyday existence of professional sports or, for that matter, a highly competitive occupation. You can't tell me a pilot is ever completely relaxed. You can't tell me a SWAT team guy is relaxed. You can't tell me a surgeon relaxes. They have relaxing moments, they have moments when the stress is more manageable than other moments, but to be an elite individual that is fully prepared and competitive, I think relaxation is a term that doesn't apply."

Be the Predator, Not the Prey

Whether it's relaxation or not, a mental state of preparedness, aggression, and readiness needs to be found. It's not letting chaos, negative thoughts, adrenaline, or anything else adversely affect performance.

Possibly the biggest obstacle in getting into the zone is fear. Fear paralyzes people. It suffocates those who do not have the tools and experience to overcome it. Fear has kept great people from expressing their greatness. Motivational speaker Les Brown, an inner-city youth who overcame great odds, says that fear is an acronym for False Expectations Appearing Real. Fear tells lies. The subconscious mind imagines all the negative possibilities and makes them greater than they really are. Fear is also a natural response.

Fear is nature at it's most basic level. Wild animals use fear instinctively, and that snaps them into predator mode. Bears have a fear when protecting their young; they use it to attack. What's scarier than a wild animal that's cornered? Both the animal and the person are scared to death. But the animal uses fear to attack; it channels everything that comes with the fear and turns it into high-intensity aggression.

The key then is to use the fear to snap into predator mode. Fear is a part of excellence. It is a powerful tool, and goes hand in hand with the imagination, one of the strongest forces on earth. Top competitors use it and harness the energy.

Tom House overcame his fear when he pitched in the big leagues with an 82 mph fastball. How scary would it be to throw an 82 mph *fastball* down the middle to someone like Barry Bonds? Now, that's fear. But House's fastball got big league hitters out for years because he didn't let fear control him.

It's similar to talking about the big game. The best coaches don't downplay the situation, rather they acknowledge that guys will be nervous, they expect it, and they welcome it. It's a part of competition. It means they're doing what those who have become stars have done—put themselves in situations where they may be nervous.

House almost embraces the feeling: "When competition is grabbing at you, at any given time from pitch to pitch, inning to inning, people want to do one of three things: they want to fight, flee, or freeze. Allow yourself to have any of those things, it makes no difference, but don't allow fighting, freezing, or fleeing to get in the way of this pitch or this swing; if you do, then you are not competing. It's OK to be afraid, it is not OK to let fear get in the way of this next pitch. If you give kids permission to have those feelings, which are normal feelings for everybody, on and off the field, they learn how to manage them. Nobody controls them, they manage them. The sooner you talk about it, the sooner you get it out in the open, and the sooner you give the athlete a mechanism by which he can manage his fight, flee, or freeze feeling, then the better he is going to be, the sooner he is going to be better."

Part of being a championship coach is knowing what the players are going through in a pressure situation and letting them know it's OK to be a little nervous, it's natural. Les Brown says he's afraid every time he speaks publicly, he'd be concerned if he wasn't afraid. But Les uses that fear; it motivates him to prepare.

Hank Aaron played in fear, and he also used it to motivate him. Going for the home run record, Aaron dealt with death threats, racial slurs, and other unimaginable pressures on top of everything else. Dusty Baker learned from him: "Hank told me you have to be nervous but never scared. You have to expect something good, you have to visualize yourself coming through."

Once a person or team learns to control their fear, they have an advantage that can take them places they've only dreamed of. Tom Trebelhorn talks about some of the common elements of his more successful teams: "My best teams were fearless. Not afraid of situations or outcomes before the event. Being able to pre-play situations before they happen so their reaction is to the play and not wishing they could do it over again. Preparedness—a good mental approach where they're ready, they're not going to let opportunities pass. When they get beat on a given night, they get beat because the pitching on the other side held them down or the other club was just hitting too much, but they're not going to very often beat themselves."

Be the Zone Catalyst For the Players

Getting players in the zone can be largely affected by the coach. His demeanor, how he acts in pressure situations, what he does when things go wrong, and how he carries himself all go into how quickly and easily players can get into their zone of peak performance.

Rod Delmonico explains: "It starts with me. If I'm tight, it transfers down. You have to stay loose as the coach. To me, they've got to see that you're confident, you're OK. The coaching staff's OK, they feel good, they feel like we're going to win, they're enjoying themselves, and don't change suddenly. If I change as the head coach, it's going to transfer down the dugout. If I usually run in this situation and I put the stop sign on, and I play very conservative and I change my philosophy offensively, they see that. Coach is tight. But if we're all out, and we're hitting and running, and it's loosey goosey...I remember in a game last year I put three hit-and-runs on in a row. They were a pretty good team. And all three worked. And I came back into the dugout and they were all excited, we scored three runs, they were pumped. I think that loosened us up that game, and we won the game and the series."

New York Yankees manager Joe Torre not only knows his X's and O's, but also, and perhaps more importantly, he knows how to get the most from each player. He is excellent at maintaining his composure during tense moments. Catcher Joe Girardi says of Torre: "Joe never panics, and you never see him berating a player. You never see him dropping his head in disgust."[7]

Jerry Kindall goes one step beyond that. Not only would he not hang his head, but he would also encourage his players. They knew that what they did on the field mattered little compared to what they did off the field. Kindall placed a heavy emphasis on the value of people versus the value of baseball: "The players know that my expectations of them are tied into their life, not to their performance on the baseball field." This helps take the pressure off his players, and put it into perspective also.

Principle #8
Excel in the Exclusive Moment

Creating players who excel in pressure situations, and the exclusive moment, is a lengthy process. It takes a lot of experience in those situations, mentally and physically. It takes being able to get into their ideal performance state when they need to so their athletic ability can take over.

These players who excel in these moments have prepared for years, perhaps their entire lives, for moments such as these. They've dreamed about them and they've used all the tools to get them into the zone—self-talk, affirmations, rituals, videos, and deep breathing all play a part in their success.

Players have, in essence, been designed for the exclusive moment. They've practiced under pressure, executed the details of the game, and gained the respect and trust of their teammates. Those teammates pushed them to continually improve, and soon they came to "live" for the exclusive moment.

Every game has a critical moment when the game is on the line and the defense needs to make a play, the pitcher needs to throw a strike, or the batter needs to get a hit. It's that single moment in the game that players need to prepare for, visualize, and look forward to; to go after voraciously—like a predator; to want it more than anything else; to dream about being the one in that position.

CHAPTER 9

Seek Greatness Through Adversity

"Everyone that is trying to accomplish something great is going to have adversity. There is no greatness without adversity. Learn from your failures. Accept your failures, not only admit them, accept them and learn from them. That is what the greatest do"

— Pat Murphy
Arizona State University

The perfect life, if one could be designed, would be filled with joy, exhilaration, companionship, love, trust, and...adversity, fear, and hardship. There can be no joy without sorrow, just as there is no love without hate, because joy conquers sorrow and love conquers hate. Without an adversary, there would be no conquering, and no need for strength. People would exist like the poor souls Roosevelt alludes to who live in the grey twilight that knows neither victory nor defeat.

Just as fear drives competitors to become more aggressive, adversity drives peak performers to summon all that is within them to compete. This is impossible without adversity, and, thus, adversity becomes the ally of the most successful people. Lance Armstrong was a top threat to win the Tour de France until he was diagnosed with testicular cancer. After getting cancer, he won the Tour de France four years in a row, not *despite* the cancer—*because of* the cancer. His cancer had become his most successful ally. "I never would have won the Tour De France without the cancer. My life is what it is because of what happened to me," he says.[1] Armstrong faced the greatest battle of his life, and defeating it gave him more strength than he ever had.

Greatness, the kind that champions ascend to, cannot be reached without adversity. Baseball is not exempt from adversity, and those who use it to their advantage win the biggest battle of all, the mental game. Champions embrace adversity and take its energy and channel it into a powerful force.

Use the Tension of Opposites

Adversity is defined as *a condition of hardship or affliction; a severe trial.* In other words, adversity is a powerful energy that tries a person to a point where they can see what they are made of. It is even described as *calamitous or disastrous.* This sort of adversity often defines a person's life: people talk in terms of "before the war," or "after the accident," or "since the trial." Their lives are often split in two: before and after an event.

Sometimes life after an adverse event becomes much greater than the prior life, in spite of the adversity. Superstar hoopster Michael Jordan was cut from his high school basketball team. A disaster for sure to a young teenager. But, as most basketball fans know, after the adversity he pushed himself and became what many people consider to be the greatest player ever.

Greatness and adversity, although seemingly opposite, are inextricably linked. The tension that results from adversity becomes the glue that brings the two to work together, complementing each other. It's like adversity is pulling on success in the opposite direction; the greater the pull, the greater the chance it will pull success off it's pedestal. In contrast, stronger pulls sometimes result in stronger rebounds and can launch people forward to greatness. Adversity is like a dangerous opportunity: two opposites that go hand in hand.

This tension of opposites is so strong, yet it is harnessed in the martial art of Tai Chi. Tai Chi is based on the concepts of the yin-yang relationship. It treats the universe as a unity. Yin and yang are opposites, but they are in unity while in opposition. In other words, opposites can work together; adversity works with success; challenging situations arise, and they can be leveraged to find even greater gain than without the challenge.

A simple example of how two seemingly disparate or adverse things may complement each other is vaccinations. In order to protect a person from disease, the body is injected with a little bit of the disease. The very thing that the body needs to fight is used as a catalyst to grow stronger. It seeks the thing it fears; uses it, confronts it, and turns it into gain.

Thus, adversity is the welcomed foundation for gain, success, and greatness. To get better, adversity must be involved. Muscles grow stronger by first being broken down. In the military, new recruits are broken down and then built up stronger. They want their new recruits to fail so they can grow. It's like pruning a tree: cutting the branches may seem painful, but the cutting allows the tree to grow and produce fruit in ways it could not without the pruning.

Pat Murphy explains the benefits of adversity: "Everybody that is trying to accomplish something great is going to have adversity. There is no greatness without adversity. Learn from your failures. Accept your failures, not only admit them, accept them and learn from them. That is what the greatest do."

Those who are able to take defeat for what it is, an experience, and learn from it are the ones who move on to greater success, whatever the situation. A defeat may be heart wrenching, it may take superhuman effort just to go on, but those who persevere use it as a springboard to propel them even further forward.

Greatness comes from working with the ups and downs as part of the game and not fighting the game and the process involved. When a player goes 0-14, he should accept it as part of the game and learn from it, knowing that all great hitters go through the same thing. That player just took on the characteristics of all great hitters; they all go through slumps, learn from them, and let them take their course.

The Value of Stress

Those people who use adversity for gain have mastered the technique allowing themselves to be pulled back by it so they can then use it to propel them forward. It becomes a push-pull thing, where life becomes a blur going backward and forward. There becomes little distinction, only in knowing that the backward pull pushes them farther forward in it's rebound.

The push and pull can be seen as stress and distress. Without stress, a person dies. He needs stimulation not only to grow, but also to exist. Stimulation and stress promote growth.

Tom House discusses the value of stress: "I talk about stress and distress. If you just look at physical preparation, the only way to make a muscle stronger is to stress it. But, if you stress it beyond its capacity, it breaks or something underneath it breaks. The same goes with the mental and emotional management of a stressful season. You have to push yourself, you have to deal with the adversity, you can't let the adversity get to a point where it becomes distressful. It's a fine line and the kid that has a broader base handles stress way better than a kid with a narrow base. I think you may have to take a step back with short-term success and start with a broader base. Then, when the kid gets that flow going, his ability to deal with stress, because of the broader foundation, is much better managed than the kid who has a very narrow base and doesn't hack it."

Greatness is a Lonely Journey

Dealing with stress is the part of competing that doesn't know win or lose, but just being on the field. Winston Churchill said, "Those who aspire to greatness must first walk alone in the desert." To be great, you've got to be willing to be defeated, and defeated means being alone; it means the willingness to risk walking alone. Those who have achieved success in pressure situations have walked alone, they have failed, and they have learned from it. There is no greatness without adversity. You may be the goat, you may be vilified, but you've got to take that chance.

One of the great leaders of the twentieth century, Nelson Mandela, walked alone. For 27 years, the South African was incarcerated as he fought for freedom. He faced adversity and was able to endure the years in prison on Robben Island because he was able to see the end result. He saw the result that few people could see. His belief that democracy would come to his country in his lifetime drove him past the obstacles, past the pressure—he dreamed it; he visualized it; he believed it; it happened.

Understanding the Nature of the Game

With the top hitters in baseball getting hits roughly 30 percent of the time, it's fairly obvious that adversity permeates baseball. The successful hitters fail over and over to get hits (not to mention the rest of the hitters), yet somehow they learn not to dwell on it. They handle the adversity as part of the game, and see it for what it is.

It is a game that is always different: the strike zone changes with every umpire, the field's dimensions are different at every venue, the mound is unique to each field, the grass may be different, the dirt, the lights, the hot dogs, everything. Basically, it is a game of uncertainty.

Ed Cheff feels that players who are the most successful are those who have a good grasp of the unpredictability of the game: "You have to understand the nature of the game. You can be real successful and fail; throw an inside fastball, saw the guy off, then it goes over the first baseman's head for a two-run double. Wait a minute, we kicked this guy's butt and he got a two-run double. So, you have to know the justices of the game. The bad hop, the bad call, the bad umpire, it's the nature of the game. Those players that can accept the uncertainty of the game go on to excel."

Cheff explains: "Life's not fair. Some five year old kid has terminal cancer, is that fair? And you're worrying about an umpire not being fair to you, and you're going, 'Man, that guy took the bat out of my hands.' Well get real, big deal, so what. I mean can't you deal with that? Don't think that everything has to be fair or everything has to be right because life's not that way—and neither is baseball. If life was fair, baseball would be fair—but it's not. Sometimes you're going to lose for some BS reasons, but there's no sense on dwelling on it. Go on to the next game. We can't do anything about yesterday, that's gone. So, we lost 10 in a row, I can't do anything about that. I just care about what we do today. Let's take care of our business today. Then, we'll worry about tomorrow when tomorrow gets here."

Define Failure

One way to look at success or failure is to look at the goal, which for many championship coaches is to win each pitch. Since this is the case, failure is only counted against that standard, not with numbers, cheers, or boos. Failure occurs then when one is not being focused in the moment, not mentally pre-playing possible scenarios, not blocking out negative thoughts, and not giving 100% effort.

Tom Trebelhorn imparts a knowledge of looking at the events in a game to his players: "I think a line drive out's not a failure. I think a hanging breaking ball hit out of the park is not failure, it's just part of the game. You're not going to be perfect all the time; they're going to have defensive players underneath some balls, you're going to get some bad calls, some bad hops, and what you have to do is keep plugging."

An important element of striving to win each and every pitch is preparing for each subsequent pitch. As Loehr mentioned, the proper emotional response to a challenging situation is the biggest part of the solution. Thus, failure can also be qualified as failure to stay positive for the next pitch.

Trebelhorn explains: "You have to maintain that the next opportunity is really the only one that matters. You can't change your strikeout, you can't change the guy jumping over the fence to catch your potential game-winning home run, the check swing blooper over the first baseman's head that beat you, or the umpire's bad call; those are all unchangeable. All we can change now is our mindset to feel better about the next opportunity we have. I think that's an important job of the manager or a leader, to maintain that perspective because the easiest thing to do is feel sorry for yourself. That's human nature. It's done with. We tend to beat ourselves up more than anybody else. We'll be complaining about things days later that 95% of baseball is not even thinking about anymore. You're the 5% worried about it. It doesn't matter, who cares, it's over. Lets try to get some of those check-swings ourselves, lets keep playing hard and we'll get lucky."

Be Good Performance Evaluators

As Trebelhorn said, it's an easy game to start feeling self-pity. A large contributing factor to this in baseball is due to players' poor self-evaluation analysis. Players look at their statistics for the game (i.e., number of hits versus number of at-bats, or number of runs allowed, etc.) and use that as a barometer, poor as it is.

Former president Andrew Jackson reportedly said, "There are lies, damn lies, and statistics." Statistics don't show how hard the ball was hit, the diving play in the hole, the extra base taken on a lazy outfielder, or the move up on a wild pitch that got four feet away from the catcher. Countless things are done on the field that are crucial to winning, but not shown in statistics.

Phil Garner actively tries to educate his players on constructively gauging their play: "We get them to be good evaluators of their performance. Players, as a general rule, are poor [at this]. We try to teach that a player who hits .250 may have had a very successful year hitting if his on-base percentage is .400. There may be another player that hit .310 but his on-base percentage was .310. The player with the .400 on-base percentage had a lot better year than the player that hit .310.

Batting average is probably the most overrated statistic in the game, and yet the measure of all hitters. Good coaches know that the true value of each statistic, and of those things that are not statistical.

Garner explains: "First and foremost, we try to get them to understand the objective with your individual stats is to help the team. Obviously, if you hit 50 home runs and drive in 150 RBIs, that helps you win ball games. But getting on base helps you win ball games. Scoring runs helps you win ball games. Being able to dive and knock down the ball with the winning run at second base when the game's on the line, that's also big."

As a coach, being a good evaluator means being able to define success. One way to define success is being able to fail over and over again without losing motivation or focus. It means being able to continually do the little things necessary for the big picture; working hard, eating right, visualizing—all the things that are easily forsaken when things aren't going right.

Dusty Baker talks about winning a championship: "It takes a lot of coming back from tough defeats. It also means staying out of sustained low periods. It takes a team that doesn't get too high when they're going good and that doesn't get too low when they're going bad."

The Third Option

One way of not allowing players to get too high or low emotionally is providing them with another option besides "winning" and "losing." This third option is "winning the pitch" (i.e., giving 100% and staying in the moment).

Bob Todd explains: "You have so many young athletes that are so conscientious and you look at some of the pressure that's on them; whether it's in the NCAA basketball tournament with millions of people watching on TV, or daily when they play. They are under the microscope, and they are 18, 19, and 20 years old. People say, 'What's going on? Why did they fail?' They didn't fail. They're conscientious. They're trying as hard as they can. So, you've got to give a kid another avenue to make sure that he protects his own ego. It's not win or lose, it's did you do everything you could to be the best you could? And then on that given day, did you do everything you could to play as hard as you can?"

Winning or losing shouldn't be based on the scoreboard. It should be based on winning the pitch. Jim Dietz sums it up: "If you approach athletics just from a winning standpoint where everything's win, win, win, then you are going to lose a lot more than you're going to win."

Find the Positives

Part of players realizing they've achieved those important moments such as keeping the ball in the infield with the winning run on second, comes with recognizing and rewarding those things. Perhaps keeping statistics on the number of blocked balls, or diving plays, or backed up bases would be more suitable things to look at.

Chuck Cottier explains: "There are a lot of positives that can come out of losing a game as a young player. The positives are: maybe you did something that helped score a run; maybe you got out of a tight situation as a pitcher, where the next time you're in the same situation, the run you're responsible for getting will be an add-on run when your ahead. Maybe getting out of a tight situation today in a loss will help you save a game when your ahead the next day. The positives always should outnumber the minuses. The one thing at the professional level you have to eliminate are mental mistakes. We all make physical mistakes, but the contending teams minimize the mental mistakes."

One way to minimize mental mistakes is to forget your blunders and remember the positives. Dusty Baker says: "Dealing with failure is probably the toughest thing to do. You never accept it but you have to deal with it. You have to turn a negative into a positive. In baseball, we deal with failure probably more than anybody in sports, because a great hitter's three for 10, so he's dealing with failure seven times out of 10. The main thing is to try and take something out of that day. Try to forget your failures and remember the good feelings, the good times that you felt, and deal with failure. You realize that nothing lasts forever. It just seems like forever when you're in the middle of it."

It's so important to see the positives because it has a major influence on self-image. With the constancy of "failure" being dealt with every day, it would be easy for a player to get down on himself, lose his confidence, and give in to the negativity facing him.

Bill Walsh had to deal with a lot of negatives in 1999 when his preseason Super Bowl favorite San Francisco 49ers had a slow start to the season. One of those negatives was the media blowing the situation out of proportion, and even calling for his dismissal. After getting crushed at home by the Philadelphia Eagles 40-8, one reporter asked Walsh, "Did you hear that, based on a poll, 80% of the fans feel you should be fired?" "Yes I heard that," Walsh replied. "What do you have to say about that?" "I'd like to thank the 20% of the people that voted for me, " he said confidently. In a seemingly bleak and negative situation, Walsh found a positive. His 49ers went on to win the rest of their games that season and the Super Bowl.

Put it in Perspective

One of the toughest things for young players to do is to keep their perspective. This comes in part from the media putting players on pedestals, giving them mass attention. Kids watch TV and they see their favorite players on the field, then in an advertisement, then at the store endorsing a shoe, the list goes on. Baseball can become the be-all-end-all, and that puts tons of pressure on young players. And with pressure comes difficulty in handling failure. However, if players are able to see that baseball is merely a game to be played for a few years, and that life encompasses much more than that, it can help players deal with the difficulties and failures they will encounter.

Legendary manager Sparky Anderson put it this way: "I always told them this: 'Look around, do you see anybody out there with a gun? Nobody's going to shoot you. You do as bad as you did today, you can do that bad tomorrow. There is nothing here in sports that is going to change your life. It will only last here until you are about 32 to 35 years old and then you are going to have to travel on to something else. So, this is just a passing fancy.' To me, sports are just a stopover; to learn about life, you learn in sports. Every day you are going to win or lose; the world doesn't come to an end."

Perseverance Builds Power

Every time a player wins, he learns a little; when he loses he learns a lot. It's like playing a game of chess; not much is learned when a lesser opponent is beaten, but play a grand master and every move is a lesson. Bob Bennett explains: "We try to get our hitters to learn from each failure. If he can stay calm and poised and stay with some intensity, he can get that."

Those who stay calm and poised through adversity become very powerful. While winning breeds confidence, winning while overcoming adversity breeds power. The player who wins despite facing adversity feels he can win against all odds. Soon, he'll stay confident, he'll stay in the moment, and he'll win the pitch against whatever opponent he faces.

The more failures a player overcomes, the more powerful he becomes. It's not how talented someone is, but how many failures it took to get where he is, that define how powerful he is. Coaches would prefer to have a player who has overcome adversity and fought hard to get to position A, than a player who's gotten to the same spot with little effort. This is because the coach knows that the player who has overcome adversity will keep fighting and keep working, and that he can be counted on when the chips are down. He also knows that player will have more inner strength and fortitude than the other player.

The player who has failed repeatedly but continually strives to improve, is winning the battle. He is doing what the top coaches are asking: he's giving 100%, and after failing repeatedly, he's refusing to feel self-pity and admit defeat. Instead, he rises up again and again, staring adversity in the face and says, "You will not defeat me."

Players who rise up again and again are hard to find. People tend to gravitate toward the path of least resistance, since it's much easier to quit than to keep going after getting repeatedly knocked down. It causes many players to fear the down time, and that stifles them.

Terry Collins explains: "The fear of failure has kept a lot of players from being great at the major league level, there's no question. Every player at this level is talented, every one of them has great skills. That fear of making a mistake, letting your teammates down, or whatever it is keeps a lot of players from succeeding. Those guys that are fearless, they're good—you win with those guys.

A player becomes fearless by facing adversity and battling through it. With a coach who supports and encourages him, he not only gains confidence in himself when he pulls through a tough situation, but he also gains confidence in he and his coach as a team. He soon becomes unafraid of making a mistake.

"One thing I try to really do is if a guy makes a mistake, to run his butt right back out there the next day. Let him know, 'Hey, that's all part of it.' This is a hard game. Offensively, it's a game of failure. It really is. That's all part of it. Not to be afraid to make a mistake, guys that take chances and are willing to stand up and be held accountable for what they did are the better players," Collins explains.

They were able to become the better player because they took a chance with their ability; they weren't afraid to lose, and this enabled them to win. Bennett says: "So, we really try to use the failure and get back up and get after it again. And that's kind of the trademark we'd like to see on our team, one that says, *You might beat us, but boy you can't beat us tomorrow.* You can beat us once, but we're going to come right back and battle you. I've always felt that's sort of like a bully that fights you. If you let him bully you every day he'll keep doing it. But, if you fight him and he beats you and he beats you and he beats you, about the fourth or fifth time he says, 'Hey, I'm getting tired of this.' That means you keep coming back at him and you finally win by just battling him, and that's what we try to do with the handling of failures."

Mike Hargrove does this: "In a game that's based largely on failure, as baseball is, you find people that absolutely can't get past the fear of failure. As far as myself, whether I've won or lost in the situation, I've been able to take away from it what I like, what I did wrong, and then completely divorce myself from it and move on."

Win the Battle of Frustration

The key in the battle of keeping battling is to avoid frustration and the accompanying negativity. It's simply a road the player's mind cannot continue down for long without losing the mental battle. He'll become distracted by other negative thoughts, and other things will cause him to lose focus. Since vividly imagined negative thoughts attract more negative thoughts, it soon spirals into a slump if not controlled.

As overcoming failure increases a player's own personal power, negativity diminishes his power. It causes him to distrust his skills, his instincts, and his luck. Bennett relates: "If [a player] starts taking the distractions and the pressure and thinking about those, he'll get negative; he'll tighten up. Then, he'll start feeling sorry for himself and not handle failure well at all."

It starts with the initial reaction to disappointment, which the better players handle with composure. Bennett continues: "The first thing [in handling failure] is to stop trying to handle it by being frustrated and showing your frustration. As though if I jumped up and down on my helmet that would cure the frustration. What we want to do is use the failure to gain success. When I lose, it's going to help me. It hurts me, but it's going to help me."

How coaches deal with their own frustration is crucial in dealing with their players' frustration. There will be times when players will choke, they won't come through, they'll lose their nerve, or they'll simply fail. That's a key moment when the coach can come in and get the player refocused and ready for his next chance. Davey Johnson explains how he handles it:

"I grew up seeing managers rant and rave when guys throw ball one, ball two, and the manager throws the helmets down the dugout. That behavior didn't just affect that starter or that pitcher; that affected nine other pitchers. Because now they're going to worry that they're going to elicit that same behavior. My style is to send somebody out, talk to him, not get upset about it. 'Look I know you're giving me the best you got, just relax, hey, don't try so hard, let's go.' (Although I'm eating Rolaids antacids and everything else.) Doug Sisk walks the bases loaded. 'Heck, get a strikeout and double play, and we're out of it.' But that's where I broke in, that's how I learned. I knew that if I didn't show confidence and I didn't give him the opportunity, he'd never be successful, would never be productive, and when I needed him, he'd get nobody out, he couldn't throw a strike. So that's really part and parcel of being a successful manager."

Show Confidence in the Players

One of the biggest ways to help players deal with failure is to maintain and improve their confidence level. With so much failure built into the game, players' confidence levels can easily plummet, and the manager plays a major role in building the self-esteem and confidence of each player.

For example, how a manager treats each player personally and professionally is very important. Does he respect his players as people first and players second? How does he react when his players fail? Does he constantly yell and scream when things aren't working? Maybe he should be yelling and screaming at himself because he didn't coach the player properly. And maybe his screaming is a manifestation of his lack of confidence or faith in how he coached his players.

If the coach shows confidence in his players verbally, and then goes against that in the heat of the moment, what good is it? Between the lines and outside the lines, the players feel more confident in themselves if their coach displays real confidence in them.

Joe Torre, manager of the New York Yankees, places an important emphasis on confidence in his players as one of his pitchers, Mike Stanton relates: "With Joe, you don't really have to look over your shoulder, because you'll lose confidence in yourself long before Joe loses confidence in you. He'll say, 'I remember what you did for me. I remember what you did for this organization. Why don't you remember?'" Hence, says Stanton, "If you're struggling, it's like, well, you're going to be right back out there tomorrow, so you better get over it."[2]

Davey Johnson knew the importance of showing confidence in his players. If the player is worried about being pulled or getting cut he's not focusing on the task at hand. Johnson goes so far as to risk his own reputation by putting some players out there that he believes in, and will "go to bat" for. When he goes that far, his players know he's in their corner, and he has confidence in them.

Johnson describes his philosophy: "I have to show them that I am confident in them. I'm the manager. I've been down that road. You're not failing, you're just experiencing some difficulties that's all. But I've got confidence in you that you can do it. Maybe you didn't do it today, but I have confidence you can do it tomorrow. And I don't want you to think if you don't do it today you won't get that opportunity tomorrow. That's where I'm putting my neck out there."

Staying on an Even Keel

Being mentally strong means being able to handle the ups and downs of baseball, and not getting too up or down. It starts with the manager. If he panics, or even shows distress nonverbally, the players will pick up on it, subconsciously maybe, but they will pick up on it. And it will show in their play. The players look to the leaders and the leaders look to the manager. If he is strong and steadfast, they can be too. It's like conditioning, if the core is weak, the extremities cannot be stable.

Mike Hargrove talks about the importance of stability: "I found that I always played better for people that weren't too up or too down. They were real consistent in what they did. So, consequently, I really try, no matter what's going on in a ball game, to keep my facial expressions the same. There are times I want to blow my top, but I sit there and I keep it inside and don't say anything. I go outside away from the fans' view, away from the camera's view, and take a player aside and talk to him there. I want them to feed off my consistency, my consistent energy, and my positivity. Because, in a long baseball season, 162 games, you can't be up and down all the time. If you are, halfway through the season you're burned out and you're a mess. You've got to stay consistent, and, when the situation demands, you spike to meet that challenge, then you come back and keep going."

Tom Trebelhorn emphasizes that as poorly as you may have played today, tomorrow is another day, and the game of your life may be just 24 hours away. So, you can't spend too much time pouting over your failures, you've got to get over them. At the same time, you've got to realize that you may have your best game of the year tomorrow and you've got to look at it that way.

Gene Mauch describes his view on adversity: "In professional athletics you don't get too carried away with a great day and you don't get too despondent over a bad day. The best hitters in the world are 70% failures. They just have to be able to handle that. If you're going to succeed as a big league player, you're going to have a certain amount of failure to overcome. The ones that have the ability to handle a certain amount of failure are the guys that materialize into outstanding big league players."

Handling failure means not letting it affect the way a player approaches the game, and the next pitch. There has to be a certain focus, and whatever happens during the course of the game, that focus should not change.

Dusty Baker explains it: "Steve Garvey's one of the best I played with for being consistent. He's a guy that I couldn't tell if he was 0-10 or 10-10. Most of the time you can tell who's ahead or who's behind by the looks on the faces, in the eyes. With Garvey, you could hardly tell one from the other. To me, that's a pro right there."

Tom House discusses the interrelation of baseball and life: "Sports is a microcosm of life. In the real world gratification is always deferred or delayed. In the sports world it's virtually instant gratification. The longest you are going to wait is until your next event. One of the things that doesn't balance off between real world and sports is that ability to deal with gratification. Failure in sports is more of an adrenaline rush than a failure in real life, so the intensity of emotion in sport, the spikes are real high, the emotions run the same gamut, but the spikes are high. In the real world, the spikes are much more spread out, the stress is spread out, it is equally strong, but it is spread out over a longer period of time. The match up is not in anything other than the level of intensity and the time involved with that intensity and the gratification of winning or losing."

Players have to go through the process to develop. They have to go through some things, some struggles, and getting through the struggles will increase their ability to handle adversity and develop the skills needed to win.

Kevin Towers discusses how you just have to go through it: "In this long of a season, everybody's going to have a period of a week or two weeks where nothing goes right. All of the sudden you start hitting and then you're not pitching, when you're pitching you're not hitting, when you're pitching and hitting you're not fielding. It happens. You just have to roll with it, try to keep the guys upbeat. And if you have some experienced ballplayers that have been through it before, they'll be good for the younger players. Let them know, 'Hey, this happens; we're going to be all right; we'll get through this and we'll get back on track.'"

When you're going through tough times, step back and smile, knowing that you're experiencing the normal ups and downs of baseball and life. And know that life is cyclical; what's here today will be gone tomorrow. And you've learned from this experience and become better for it.

Jerry Kindall not only knew what his players were going through, but he also actively sought to empathize with and relate to them that he had been there, and that it's OK to fail once in a while. Kindall explains: "We address adversity with verbal encouragement. To help them overcome those moments of failure, and there's so many of them, I think it's helpful if the coach has been there, to experience the failure, to know what it's like to be struck out in the ninth inning with the bases loaded. I'm very open about my failures as a baseball player. I want them to know that I understand their heart and their emotions when these things happen to them. When you fail, you think that the whole world sees it, the whole world knows and scorns you; it's not true. But that's an adolescent reaction to failure."

Dealing With the Slump

Jim Leyland spent 18 years in the minor leagues before he began his big league career as a manager. He has dealt with as much failure as anyone and that's why he has had so much success. He's seen many slumps come and go over the years.

He explains how he deals with them: "I don't care how good you are, you'll go into a slump. I don't care how bad you are, you'll win some games. I think the peaks and valleys you have to be careful of, you ride those out. You don't get too excited, you don't get too high or too low. You've got to stay on some form of an even keel even though it's hard.

"And the other thing is that you rest people. A lot of times people think when you take a guy out your resting him physically, but a lot of cases your resting him mentally—to get away from it. He's struggling, he's fighting, it doesn't matter what he's doing he can't get a hit, he can't make a pitch. Every now and then you have to get people away from it. And, obviously, you can't tell them to go home for two or three days, but you say, 'Hey, set you down for a couple days, get away from it, clear the cobwebs, don't take batting practice, do whatever you want to do.' I think that's important. It's a long grind."

Ed Cheff reminds his players that even the best ones go through down times. That doesn't mean they're no longer the best he says: "Once a great hitter, always a great hitter. Once a great shortstop, always a great shortstop. So what, you made three errors in the last three games but, 'Hey, you're a great shortstop.' You wouldn't be playing if you weren't a great player. If you weren't a really good hitter I wouldn't be hitting you. I don't jerk them around and change the order quick, and panic and knock them down to eight hole or something. If you did it before, you'll do it again, it's just a matter of time."

Knowing that it is just a matter of time and refusing to panic is what the veterans do. Tom House uses Paul Molitor as an example: "If you prepared yourself properly, slumps don't last as long. I heard Paul Molitor say it perfectly when someone asked him, 'What is the difference between hitting .325 at the age of 40 and hitting .325 at age 20?' and he said, 'The only difference is that I make my slumps less.'"

He gave in to the fact that there's going to be slumps. He didn't allow the slump to create a critical mass and control him, he let it run its course knowing full well that it would work itself out. Youngsters have the tendency to panic, leave their preparation foundation and start chasing their tail. Slumps are going to happen, it's a given. If you are fully prepared and confident in that preparation, then the slumps will be less, according to Paul Molitor. You are still going to have them, but you don't start changing to try to fix the slump at the expense of the preparation. The fix is in the preparation, not the slump," House explains.

Slumps are a part of baseball. They are inevitable to even the greatest players—a natural and unavoidable part of the game. The first key to dealing with slumps is to know that they are an integral part of every player's season and career.

The first thing to do when things aren't going right is to take a time-out. Like a basketball coach whose team just gave up five straight baskets, a player can take a time-out to get refocused, and get momentum back on his side. Time-outs can last a few seconds or a few days.

After taking a time-out, it is a good idea to analyze the source of the slump. Slumps may have physical causes (injuries, over-training, vision problems, etc.), psychological causes (feeling the pressure to continually excel, wondering why you never get any breaks, etc.), or technical causes (Bobby Bonilla adjusting his stance after being told he was a bit farther away from the plate than normal in the 1997 World Series). It's important to identify the cause of the slump before a remedy is prescribed.

The next step is to go back to the process goals involved with winning the pitch. Things such as daily training goals (i.e. take 100 extra swings a day, do 50 extra sit-ups, etc.), and daily performance goals for each game (i.e., running every ball out hard, walking tall no matter what, etc.).

For example, if a player is struggling at the plate and hasn't gotten a hit since the Reagan era, then some action may need to be taken. Getting away from the game may help, then analyzing tape (if there is any) of his swings, and looking back at the swings when he was doing well and comparing the two. He may be anxious and be pressing.

If this is the case, as it so often is, the coach may say, 'OK, I want you to come early for batting practice the next three days and we're going to work on going the other way.' So, the coach throws him pitches on the outside half and the batter works on hitting the ball the other way. Maybe he then sets a goal of taking 100 extra swings (in groups of 5 to 10 or 12 optimally) working on driving the ball the other way. He then sets a goal of running every ball out 100%, and maybe another goal of holding his head high after each at-bat, no matter what. He might even have someone on the bench watch his at-bats and tell him if he swung at any balls that weren't strikes, or anything else he may have seen. He may even keep his own little chart on each pitcher (if he knows he'll see the pitcher again). The chart can be as simple as what pitches he has, what's his best pitch, how his control is, any tendencies he may have, his move to first, and his pace or tempo; he may also note his velocity.

Ed Cheff has had success with his players because he doesn't let little things turn into big things. When a player has a problem he addresses it, and if it's a problem on the field he'll take that player out, one-on-one, and work on it until it gets straightened out. He says: "I like to deal with it (a slump) on an individual basis; if my shortstop's having some trouble, he and I will go out, just he and I. And if I have a hitter that's having some troubles, just he and I. I think the attention is good for him and I feel good that I tried to do something for him. I feel good about it and he feels good about it and maybe we figured something out. Shoot, I might have told him something, probably didn't mean anything, but it might have done something up here for him. Then, you hope he goes out and gets a hit the first time up the next game, and he thinks you're real smart and you think you're real smart.

Encourage, Support, and Time Off

For Jerry Kindall, he lessens player slumps through encouragement, support, extra work, and time off when needed: "Normally, to get a guy out of a slump you increase the practice time and you increase the support. Encourage him and reduce the criticism to love him out of that slump. So, you increase the repetitions. Now, there is time where you just have that guy rest; just take a break. But, most of the time you increase repetitions. But, I think most important is to be loving, supportive and encouraging to a guy who's in a slump."

Terry Francona makes sure his players are taken care of when they need help: "First of all, you try and make sure you have instructors there all the time to help them. Second thing is, you don't turn your back on them. When they're struggling, as long as they're giving you an effort, you have a responsibility of being there for them. Not to yell at them, nobody wants to go 0-4, but to be there for them, to encourage them, to help them. That's what we try to tell them all the time, 'Hey, if you bust your butt, we'll be there for you. We'll try to help you.'"

Remember the Successes

One thing that players seem to quickly forget when things are going tough is all the successes they've had. They remember what they haven't done, not what they have. It's important to remember, like Cheff says, that once a great player, always a great player. There should be things available for a player to go back and picture the great things of the past, the successes. The good things should be recorded, via video tape, photos, newspaper articles—everything that adds to the picture of success.

Bob Bennett explains: "When a player is in a slump, I like them to go back, forget about failing, and look at all the things they've done well. If you've got a scrapbook, go back and brag about yourself through that scrapbook. 'Boy, I'm good. I did a good job here, look I was all-league there.' I want to present as good a picture to myself as I can and I don't want to see any bad things. The trouble with a slump is we only see the bad things. We don't remember the good things. We just think, *Gosh, I'm uncomfortable at the plate, I can't swing, I'm having trouble, nothing falls in…* if I could only turn that around and say everything good is going to happen to me, you'd get out of the slump."

Rod Delmonico uses videotape to remind his players of their past success: "We go back to watch tape of when they were doing it well. I think it's really important for them to see themselves visually doing it well. We try to make it simple. Hit the ball back up the middle, go the other way. You go back to the basics. Sometimes, we'll go back and work on their bunting. But we'll go back and watch tape. Usually, it's a physical thing, unless the guy has hit the ball on the nose four games in a row and then starts changing things."

Experience Helps Players Get Through Failure

Part of being human is learning from those who've gone before us. Having parents and coaches who've been in the same position enables the younger generation to learn from their mistakes and be prepared for them. Every single problem, slump, challenge, and obstacle a player is facing has been faced, and overcome, by someone before. Having a mentor can be an incredible help to inexperienced players. It's just like anything, whether you're a businessman getting help from a retired CEO, or a player learning from an ex-big leaguer, the experience is there to be had. And the benefit is obvious.

Having players and/or coaches who have been through the war, the trenches, gives players a foundation to lean on, to watch and learn from. If a rookie sees a veteran going through a prolonged slump and dealing with it, he can learn how to do the same. A good example is Ryne Sandberg, one of the great second basemen to play the position. He was well-known for having slow starts. He'd be hitting close to the Mendoza line in April and the untrained baseballer may question him. But, if they were to look at previous years, they would see that he always comes back to overcome that. So, a rookie watching him in April could learn from his confidence.

Charlie Blaney explains: "Having the people there with them who have experienced it; they're really the best teachers. The coaching staff we have, everyone who's gone through it has experienced it. That's probably the biggest hurdle a young player has to overcome. Going from being the star of his team in high school or college, to being one of 25 former stars. Where you used to hit home runs in high school or college, now you're striking out. You used to throw shutouts, now you're getting hammered if you're a pitcher. Everyone has to overcome that. So, our staff knows that, they are tuned in to that, and they are sensitive to that."

A player's own experience with failure is a key factor in learning to deal with failure in the future. If a player struggles and struggles and comes out of it, it will help him in the future when he encounters something similar.

Tom Kelly explains: "Everybody has to fail. You're going to fail if you're the hitter 7 out of 10, sometimes more than that. So people that handle that, they're going to be much more successful because their head is going to stay screwed on correctly. Keeping their head focused and screwed on right comes with experience; a lot of young guys are going to fail. Sometimes it's difficult for them, and they have to go back and work on things. They're usually much better off when they come back the second time around. Because they have to experience the failure and go out and get some help."

The best players may have an ingrained ability to deal with failure and not take it personally—to ignore the negatives and see the positives, or learn from the negatives and remember the positives.

The Fear of Success

The ability to be persistent, to keep battling when all odds are against you is one of the true trademarks of a champion. Some players have an ingrained idea of how good they are, and how good they might be. This propels them to get up when everyone else stays down. It's a drive inside of them, a relentless desire to overcome all obstacles to be the best they can be. Whether it's nature or nurture, the best players are indomitable. It may be an innate fear of reaching their potential. The fear of looking back on their life and wondering, *How good would I have been if I'd only…* or the fear of not being responsible to themselves to use all their potential, all their talent.

W. Somerset Maugham said: "It's a funny thing about life: If you refuse to accept anything but the very best, you will very often get it." Some people, great people, are afraid that they will accept less than what they can be or do, and that drives them to be better. As legendary football coach Lou Holtz said, "Mediocrity is unacceptable when you are capable of doing better."

Kevin Towers explains his approach to dealing with failure: "There are players that have fear of failure, and players that have fear of success. And usually the guys that end up having long, long careers have the fear of success. Failure's going to happen. What I like are guys that have a fear of how good they might be. They know they're good, but they know they might be the next Ty Cobb, and you got other guys that are always waiting to fail. And usually, those guys end up out of the game fairly quickly… Guys that have fear of success, [think], *How good might I be? Boy, I reached this, so now how good might I be?* There are other guys that are just waiting for something bad to happen. It's part of the game and how you deal with it, how you deal with adverse situations, how mentally strong you are."

Principle #9
Seek Greatness Through Adversity

There is greatness in adversity because it is a very powerful force. Adversity causes fear and fear causes many people to lose out on what could have been because they were afraid. It strikes down very strong men, cripples them, and many never recover. Those who do become powerful. They've taken the power of adversity and refocused it for their own ends.

Along the way to greatness it's often a lonely journey. Most lesser mortals will drop off, succumbing to the negativity brought on by doubt, fear, and failure. Those who persevere, those who take the energy in the stress, those who get accustomed to the adversity and learn how to handle it go on to count themselves among the few who had the courage to overcome the obstacles on the path to their dream.

They've learned to be good evaluators of their performance, knowing the nature of the game and the built-in failure, to see the good and handle the rest. Those who don't rechannel the energy are easily distracted by the barrage of negativity that comes with an unfocused mind. Without staying focused on the task at hand, on each pitch, negativity will creep in.

As Bob Bennett says, success is on the far side of failure: "Failure is everywhere and so are distractions. Those are the two toughest things you deal with in the game of baseball. They're just exactly like what you deal with in life. We talk about mental toughness and the ability to get up from failure. The success of every player will depend on how he handles failure."

CHAPTER 10

Motivate Daily

"To me, you can go out and take ground balls and you can hit, but if you don't touch the mental part every day…it's not happening. You have to motivate every day. It's the most important thing I do."

— Rod Delmonico
University of Tennessee

Champions are very motivated because the things they do provide a framework that cultivates motivation. They have an uncommon discipline to do those things necessary to succeed. As they continually do the things that they know will help them get better, that motivates them. Building a life around excellence is motivating. Having a clear purpose and covenant, continually visualizing the end result, and developing trust and respect among teammates are all very motivating.

Champions are disciplined to do the little things that keep them focused in the moment which prepares them to excel in the exclusive moments. They learn to embrace adversity and use it as an ally. They push themselves to practice every day with intensity, and they are masters at using adversity to their advantage. Each of these things builds on the other, and it creates an energy that becomes a force.

Each individual is unique to what motivates him the most, and that's where the coach identifies and targets it. Sometimes a breakdown in any of the nine other principles means motivation is needed. Players need to be motivated to follow the principles outlined in this book, and when they do, they become self-motivated, which is the goal. It comes down to where each player learns the discipline to form a solid framework (of which the 10 principles are the base) to maintain motivation to continually excel.

Develop an Atmosphere of Common Purpose

Internal motivation starts with having a purpose, which can be outlined in a covenant. Just as the media constantly bombards the public from every angle (e.g., radio, TV, billboards, newspapers, magazines, etc.), the coach can flood his players with the core covenant from every angle. The playbook, the words he uses, his actions, the locker room, posters on the wall, motivational speakers, videos, stories, are all ways to continually try to develop the common purpose—a common purpose of being committed to the team's goals and values.

Jerry Kindall used the locker room as a sanctuary to motivate his players. There he got his players committed to a common theme that pulled them together. He explains: "We reminded the players of the successes of the past in the locker room; we had pictures up and the pennants and the colleges, and so on. So, visually when they walked in the locker room, they saw a neat locker room, they saw reminders of past performances, championships, great players; it was our little sanctuary. We used the locker room to develop the ingredient of a common purpose."

Bob Todd tries to create an atmosphere that excites and motivates the players to come to the park and work hard. He explains: "My assistants and I work hard to create an atmosphere that our players are going to enter every day that motivates and where they want to motivate themselves."

Ed Cheff's teams are highly motivated but perhaps in a different way than some of the other teams. He gets his teams to pull together, push each other, compete, have courage, all the necessary ingredients to win, but he does it without a locker room. Cheff has a common purpose of intensity of will, and that high energy, that burning desire and aggression more than makes up for the lack of togetherness a locker room can bring.

See Their Perspective – Know Where They're Coming From

Creating a motivating atmosphere takes having an idea of what the players are going through and what they've been through. If motivation is defined as providing a stimulus to act, then relating to a player is the spark to light the fire. When a coach understands a player's background, then he can find out what makes him tick.

The challenge is to get close enough to the players to do that, while still maintaining the player/coach relationship. There has to be good communication in order to do that in a sincere, caring manner. Care is important while maintaining respect so the players know there's a line they can't cross.

Davey Johnson explains what he does: "I think you have to be close enough to know where they're coming from. If you're not aware of what they're having to deal with, then you're not paying attention and you're not going to be a good manager. If you're aware how you can help them and how the coaches can help them, then it's always from a positive standpoint, and mainly showing confidence in the players, mainly being positive. Those things are very critical."

Understanding how to help a player means knowing his thought process, and when this occurs, then there's a certain measure of respect. Dusty Baker knows how to get close to his players yet maintain enough distance to lay down the law when necessary: "I think that I'm young enough where I can relate to these dudes, in music or whatever. The fact that I don't always have to tell you that I'm the boss, I think that is number one. I try very hard not to embarrass them in the paper or in public. I try extremely hard to be honest with them."

Johnson relates: "To get the respect of your guys, you have to get down there and get dirty with them; you can't just give orders to them to go dig up the ditch and you aren't helping them. I think that's big."

Rod Delmonico works hard to find out all he can about how his players' minds work: "We test every one of our kids every year so I have a great idea of what makes them tick. We have a testing system to test how competitive they are; will they play in pain; are they a team player; what is their attitude, it has a wide variety of things. I think it's important for me to prepare myself to get ready, so I've got a wide variety of info to give them, and understand the mental part of the game."

Mike Hargrove says that to be a good manager you've got to both empathize and be the boss, and to draw those together in such a way that the players respect and listen to you. He explains: "I think you have to try to understand and maybe empathize with what a player is going through and what a player feels, but at the same time, you have to understand that you have to have a certain amount of toughness, maybe cold-heartedness to be able to make decisions, that while they may be unpopular to a certain player, they really are to the benefit of that player and the team. They have to understand from your point, that there are tough decisions that you have to make, and that's just the way it is. So you mix the two in that regard. It seems to work."

Dusty Baker wants to empathize with his players, to walk in their shoes. He wants total honesty from his players and in return he does the same: "I have rules. I have personal rules for my team, and the organization has rules. The organization has rules that can be about facial hair, clothing on the road, plane rules, whatever. My rules are basically very simple: do not lie to me, give me a chance to understand. My second rule is: show up to work on time. If you cannot do that then give me a call, but just do not call me too often with the same excuse. My other rule is don't embarrass yourself or the organization or your teammates, and if you have a squabble with somebody, me or anybody else, we'll get it out in the open. I learned that in the military, don't let it fester. Take care of it right away and try to do it behind closed doors, one-on-one, unless that person chooses that particular forum out there, which I try not to do. I try not to embarrass guys in front of other guys because it happened to me when I was playing and I never forgot it. I disliked it immensely. I said I'd never treat anybody like that. Another rule is: don't go to the newspaper with any comments or squabbles about somebody. Go to that person in person, don't talk behind anybody's back. That's about it. Also, no off the field injuries; don't come in with banged up elbows from skateboarding, surfing or rollerblading. Realize that this is your job; other than family and God this is the most important thing in your life these next eight months, in our lives, and to each other. If you do not do that, you are not only letting yourself and your family down, you're letting God down and your teammates down."

Get Close Enough to Understand Them in Order to Motivate

Managers must not only relate to their players, but get them to translate the goals, the core covenant, and the detail coaching into action. The coach can have all the knowledge in the world about how to win a championship, but if he can't communicate, what good is it? He has to know how to translate his knowledge of the game into their application of that knowledge. Good communication skills are essential for this.

Good communication starts with mutual respect between the players and coaches. It's not necessarily a buddy-buddy thing, but a joint belief that the players can win and that the coach can lead. That comes from relating to players.

Terry Collins says: "Some players I get real close to; others it's hard to. I want to make sure they understand they can talk to me about anything. Whether it's where they hit in the lineup, how I used them the day before, anything. I don't go out with them, but I don't mind having dinner with them once in a while. I really believe in this day and age, you have to be closer to your players than you were years ago.

"Since there are a lot fewer good players today than there were years ago, you have to make sure that they're in your corner. And they need to know that you're in theirs. I preach and preach and preach that we all wear the same uniform. We're all on the same side of the rope. If they understand and believe that, you'll have their respect, and they'll play hard for you. You can say what you need to say with them knowing that you don't mean to hurt their feelings, you're just trying to make them better," Collins explains.

Terry Francona discusses his relationship with his players: "I do get very close to my players; and I don't try not to. Sometimes it hurts a little bit when things go wrong, and you have to make decisions, but it's fun being around the players, and I don't try to hide that. I like them."

Phil Garner says: "I think I'm fairly close. Do they tell me their marital problems or girlfriend problems? Probably not, but I think I have a pretty good feel for them. I think all my players feel if they had something to tell me, they'd tell me. I think they have a feeling that they are close enough to me that I would help them; I think most of them know that if it's something that I could do that I would do it.

Ed Cheff has an interesting relationship with his players. Known as one of the most intense coaches in the game, he demands intensity from his players. And his players recognize that he knows how to win. He may be tough, he may be intense, and he wins. He doesn't win just being tough, he has the ability to communicate effectively to his players.

Cheff explains: "My players tell me it's kind of a love-hate type thing: they really like me some days, and other days they hate me. I'm really at odds with guys sometimes, and then I'm really close to them. I'm kind of abrasive to them at times, but I kind of turn that off, off the field."

Dusty Baker relates to his players as well as anybody. He describes how he is with his players: "Pretty close. It is impossible not to get close to them and get the most out of them, because you'll never understand them. The hard part about that is when you have to say goodbye at some point. But you hope you've had a positive impact on their life."

"I learned the most about meshing in the marines. Just try to get them to pull in the same direction as soon as possible. Let's face it, we are going to be together for eight months, with maybe one or two days off a month. For that period of time these are your friends, whether you like it or not. Then when the season's over you can choose your own friends."

Jim Leyland molds a team concept by personality: "You handle each player differently, yet you handle each player the same. Some guys you can leave alone, you don't have to ever worry about them. Other guys you need to touch them up from time to time, you need to lay a little challenge out there for them. And you have fun with them; I had a lot of fun with this championship team."

Leyland takes the opposite approach from some coaches in relating to his players. He's close to them on the field but not off: "I'm close in the clubhouse but not after that, because I think they need to get away from me, and I need to get away from them. But in the clubhouse I'm very close to them; on the field and in the clubhouse, I love the players. I love to be around the players, but they need their private time and I need mine."

Relating to players is crucial to be successful as Leyland underlines: "It takes patience handling your players. Knowing how to handle them as individuals and yet as a team. Obviously, all major league managers know the strategy of the game, so I believe it's your ability to relate to your players that gets the most out of them."

Tom Kelly talks about how he relates to his players: "You have to draw the line. I like to play cards together. We fool around a little bit, banter about. But within that, you have to draw some kind of line. I'm the boss and I'm going to run the show, that sort of thing. But there doesn't have to be this big line that says, 'Hey, I'm here and you're there.' You can be one of the boys and still be the boss."

Tom Trebelhorn explains: "I'll play golf with them, chat with their wives. I don't try to be aloof or best buddies, but I think it's a long season and you have to certainly be sociable, and if there are things we mutually like to do, I do them with the players. It's kind of like if our interests coincide, we'll go do something, if they don't nothing to it. See you at the park, no problem. But I don't put hotel bars off limits, they can go in hotel bars where we're staying, I don't care. They just have to behave themselves. And just as I won't do anything that would embarrass them, I expect them not to do anything to embarrass me, whether it's on a professional level or a social level."

Baker describes what it was like to play for Tommy Lasorda: "He was cool with us. We used to go out as a team. He would take us out to dinner, maybe come to a nightclub with us sometimes and have a couple drinks with us. Sometimes he was a boss, and sometimes he was one of the fellas. If we got too far out of line and he was one of the fellas, he was the boss again. That was cool with me."

Ed Cheff tries to be very up front with his players: "If there's a problem, we try to be real clear with it, we try to keep the avenues of communication open. I'm very open, I like a lot of open communication. If I'm not happy with you, I'll tell you and your teammates. I want everybody to know how you and I are getting along; I don't want to be phony with it."

Jerry Kindall is more stern on the field and more personal off the field: "On the field, players would say I was rather aloof. I had this structure, I had the practice plan, and I wanted to stick with it. On the field, I was kind of no nonsense. It's how I operated, how I coached. Good or bad, I couldn't change it. Off the field, I definitely wanted to get close to my players. I wanted them to know that I cared, to know that I would be glad to be with them and counsel them for problems other than baseball, as well as baseball."

"My wife was a terrific friend for the players too. We always had the new players over for dinner at the start of the year and the seniors at the end of the year. The best way to get close to your players is to just be available to them, to let them know that they're number one. They know that whenever they want to come see me in the office, they take priority. The president of the University could be in there, and if somebody needs to come in and see me about an important item in their life, I will excuse myself and see them. They are most important," Kindall explains.

"The other thing that helps them understand that I am not just a coach but a person that would like to be available to help them is how I treat my children, how I treat my wife. They see that they are more important than success in baseball. My wife comes first, my children come next, and my players are part of my family. So if I treat my wife and children with love and respect, and honor them, the players then have reason to believe I will do the same to them. We call our baseball program 'the baseball family.' So if somebody screws up in the family, that impacts all of us. Somebody gets in trouble in the dorm, or flunks out it's a reflection on all of us."

Get Players to Believe in Themselves

The learning curve of young players is such that they don't know how good they can be, and coaches may not either. They may have a better idea, but nobody knows for sure what they'll do in the coming year. But treating them as if they will still be tomorrow what they are now will surely limit them. So to get players to reach their (untapped) potential, you've got to treat them as if they already are what they could possibly be, what you dream they might be.

Kevin Towers believes in this philosophy: "I think the best motivation is to continually be positive and praise people for good work they do. Even if it's something very, very small and very minute. I always look at the way I was treated as a young scout or as a young player, and the people that I benefited most from were the people who were the most positive. Tom House was a guy that always made you feel like you had a chance to pitch in the big leagues, even if you probably didn't. But I always seemed to excel in those years. I was around people that were positive that always made you believe or at least made you feel that your were doing something right, and even if you did something wrong, they tried to turn negatives into positives. I would say a motivational tool for me is to always build on the positives, and if there are negatives, to try to turn negatives into positives, in a positive way."

For Tom Trebelhorn, possibly the number one thing he does is get players to believe in themselves. He explains: "I try on a player by player basis to get every guy feeling better about themselves, and feeling better about the team, even if its just for a few days."

For Towers, his biggest role as a general manager is managing people, getting them all to take ownership of the team. He really makes his players feel like they are a significant part of the team, even if their role is the most insignificant. That's what many of the top managers do. Towers explains: "I think if people enjoy what they're doing, people feel like they're a part of something, they're going to go the extra mile for you. And they're going to be motivated every day to help out and do things because they think their input means something."

Davey Johnson motivates his players with an integrity such that players know he will go to bat for them, and if says he believes in you, he'll make you believe it. "[My most important role as manager is] fighting for the guys that I know will be able to do some things that need to get done during the course of the year. Guys that, if I think that you're going to succeed or fail, you want to give them the opportunity to help you succeed or fail. Whether it's a guy like Jeff Reboulet, who when Alomar was out played great (in 1997)—a gamer, a lot of heart, a workaholic, not a lot of talent. Does he run fast? No. Can he hit the ball hard? No. Can he catch it? He can catch it, he can throw it, he can play a couple positions. But he's giving you all he's got, he'll be grinding up there mentally, he'll get you a big hit occasionally. He'll end up hitting .230, but he's a winner. You have to identify that, and that's important as a manager.

"You try to treat each guy the same, but, by and large, each guy's earned a different treatment," Johnson explains. "And each guy wants a different treatment. It might be caring about a guy having chemo, and how I can be a part of establishing that he's OK for the next year or whatever, giving him the chance to be a part of the team again. Or, for a reliever that's been booed two or three times, keep bringing him back out so when I need him he's available. Those are invaluable things that a manager has to deal with, and if you don't, you lose these different players when you need them most. So, it's the handling of a player during the bad times. Anytime a player's going good he doesn't need a lot of handling."

Get the Motivation to Come From Within

Players need to find ways to motivate themselves every day. Scouting director Terry Wetzel explains how important that is: "We are looking at the makeup of the player and [wondering if he is] a self-motivator. What does the high school or college coach have to use to motivate the player? Hopefully, not a whole lot. Baseball is a long season, you play 162 games. You better be self-motivated or you are not going to be successful."

Pat Gillick has won because he knows talent, and he knows what kind of athlete he's looking for. He explains: "If you have the right athletes, you don't have to motivate them, they're already motivated. Those kinds of athletes are motivated by pride, there's something inside of them that says, *You're not going to get in front of me, you're not going to be better than me. I am better than you and I will show you that I'm better than you.* What you do for those athletes is, put them in the lineup and let them play. And you wish you had a whole bunch of them. You wish you had every player like that."

Getting players to be able to provide their own stimulus to train and practice hard, and do what needs to be done is something coaches strive for. When they can motivate themselves even when they don't feel motivated, great things can be done.

That's where successful athletes separate themselves from the rest. They are able to motivate themselves when it's January, and it's raining, and they have to go for a run outside or play long toss or whatever.

Bennett explains: "We try to get the motivation to come from within. That's through the goal setting we talked about. Everybody comes to the ball park with different feelings. There are three moods you come to the park with. It's up to you to correct and adjust how your mood is before you ever get into the locker room. Some days we come, we're ready to go, and we don't need a speech or anything. That's about a third of the time. The other two-thirds of the time I'm going to either be slightly off of that or a lot off of that, in degrees. So I have to check myself. If I come in and I'm a little lazy, I have to have some kind of little system I can kick in to get myself activated. Usually, if I'm just a little bit lazy, all it takes is to give myself just a little chalk talk or do a little running and I'm ready to go again. The third way is when I'm really off, and that takes a lot of work. What we want each player to do, and we harp and harp on this, is to look at yourself every day and evaluate, 'How am I? Am I motivated?' If I'm not, I have to motivate myself. Every great player has done this. He gets himself ready. That's the first step.

"The second step," Bennett says, "is to contribute to getting the team ready. And the team might have a completely different mood than he has. So, it's the job of everybody to say, 'Here's the mood we need to be in—a highly motivated mood—and we have to help each other get there. We use all kinds of things to do it. I write a lot of poetry, and I use poetry to motivate on a daily basis. We have stories we tell to motivate. Bertman does a good job with video. Mine is through poetry and talks."

Bob Todd gets his players to share his energy and be self-disciplined: "It's critical that you're enthusiastic, that those players have to work hard. They've got to reach for common goals. There are individual goals and then there are common goals. I think in the more successful programs, the leadership is gearing it toward a certain discipline, but they are trying to get the athlete to be self-disciplined.

"That's the ultimate goal, for athletes to become self-disciplined. When you have athletes that are self-disciplined and self-motivated, then the coach needs to step back, get away, and just let them go because they will head in the right direction. They are going to end up eating the right kinds of foods. They'll end up understanding what's right and wrong and do the little extras that it takes to win and not cheat anybody," Todd explains.

When you get players who are self-motivated, they lead by example and focus intently on the team concept and the necessary actions to get the goal accomplished, while bringing others along.

Leaders on the Team Motivate and Police Others

One of the most important avenues of motivating players is through peer support and motivation. If you can get a few leaders on the team to buy into the team concept, the goals, the core values, and mode of operation, then the players will regulate themselves to a large extent. When they do, the team stands a great chance of really coming together and reaching their potential.

A coach can tell a player to work hard and it helps, but the coach is only one guy and he's not there but a few hours a day. The players see each other all day long, (i.e., in class, at practice, after practice, at the sock-hop, whatever). If the leaders on the team keep the other guys focused on the big goal, then there's much greater cohesion and unity.

Pat Gillick explains: "You have to have three or four guys that can motivate their peers during the course of the season. Management can say things to the players, help the players, but it takes a peer to really get on other players, and get other players motivated and headed in the right direction. It's very important in the clubhouse to have some people that can take charge of the club. Guys like [Cal] Ripken, Joe Carter, Eric Davis, etc. Guys who are kind of take-charge guys in the clubhouse, sort of coaches in themselves, without being officially designated. If you want to, call them captains. But there has to be a group of players who can appeal to the players, get on the players, and keep the players headed in the right direction if you do run into tough times."

Jerry Kindall has his players nominate captains who do a lot to motivate and encourage their teammates in conjunction with the coach but also where he isn't able: "We depend a lot on our captains to encourage their teammates. There are long sessions in the weight room, and long sessions conditioning, and our players get tired and get discouraged.

"I have a weekly meeting with the captains. We say, 'How are we doing? Who's dragging? What can we do together to help him get on top of it?' Then they'll say, 'Well, so and so's girlfriend dumped him, that's why he's blue.' But, at the same time, we tell them what we can do to help our team together," Kindall says.

Bob Bennett encourages a culture of peer support and leadership on his teams: "We keep a fine eye on players, and make sure they don't get distracted during the season. That takes constant and vigilant watching. Each player keeps track of himself and we want the peer pressure from the team to do it also. Because they're more powerful with each other than I am. If you have five or six leaders on the team that say, 'Hey, knock that crap off,' it's better than having the coach say it. Because you can fool the coach, you can't fool the players."

The power of peer motivation can be looked at in the following manner. The coach will lay out certain parameters for the team to follow regarding practices, workouts, team representation, etc. Then the leaders on the team will decide how they will act upon it. They will influence the majority of the team by how much they buy into the program's ideals, the coach, and their desire to win.

When given a clear direction from the managers, players can excel and bring out their own greatness if they are allowed to express themselves and let their excellence flourish. What happens is that players see that the coach believes enough in them to respect their space and their ability as adults to take care of business, and they respond. If the coach is spending a lot of time babysitting his players, then he's not coaching.

Dusty Baker relates so well to his players partly because he gives them the leeway to police themselves. In fact, he encourages them to do so, and to lead by example. He explains: "I think motivation comes from within. You have to have leaders on the field. It's easier for another player to motivate than for a coach to motivate. I can have all those knock-down-drag-out meetings, but I cannot tell them you cannot do this thing or the other. I have players on the field, hopefully in the infield, a leader at the catching position, and a leader in the bullpen. I need a leader on the pitching staff and a leader on the bench, players who are not afraid to police themselves because I think a primary source of motivation for these guys is for them to police themselves and not necessarily have me to police them. Because when I have to police them, then it becomes disciplinary most of the time. If you can police yourselves, then go ahead and do it, and if you can't, that's when I have to come in."

When players are extremely gifted, they often feel confined by the rest of their peers, teachers or coaches. It's important to let them use their gifts and not limit their ability to do this, while still maintaining the boundaries of the team. One way to do this is to place the burden of policing themselves directly on the players, and then to lead by example. Show them how to motivate themselves, and let them do it. They may need supervision, but if they can take the lead and run with it, they may be able to show you things you didn't know were possible.

High Energy and Optimism

A big part of stimulating self-motivation is to bring an enthusiasm and energy to the team that is contagious. Smile at someone and they'll be hard pressed not to smile back. Do something extra for the team and someone else will follow suit. It's just how the universe works.

Tom Trebelhorn explains his philosophy: "In general, be organized and demonstrate high energy and optimism at all times. You'll be alright. If you're organized and you're optimistic with high energy, players will really play well for you. And they'll enjoy playing for you, and they'll keep coming to play for you, and word will get out, and you'll get other players because guys will say, 'This guy's fun to play for.' I think if you do that, if you're organized, have high energy, and your optimistic, then I think you have a chance; I think if it's a fun environment, that's the way games should be."

Part of having high energy often means getting your nose in there, getting dirty with the players. It lets them know that you're not above doing the work that needs to be done (i.e., working on the field, cutting the grass, whatever).

Videos and Stories

One of the most immediate and inspiring motivational tools is video. Skip Bertman's renowned use of videos has inspired thousands of players to be their best. Winning five out of 10 national championships in the 1990s era speaks to the fact that, Bertman's use of videos works for him. He plays a video before every game, usually a short video of great plays from the past, championship teams winning it all, and shots of Omaha where the national championship is always played. This puts images in the players' minds of exactly where they want to go, what it looks like, what it feels like, and what it smells like. Bertman's combination of videos and story telling has propelled him to legendary status.

Gary Adams at UCLA integrates story telling and acting into his motivational arsenal. He'll dress up to tell a story, and he'll act out a story. He feels that if they can get a good picture in their minds (and maybe have a laugh and remember it well), then the idea is going to stay with them. He explains: "Sometimes you have to do crazy things to get your players' attention. The most important thing is being enthusiastic and eager and getting your players to believe that it's important to you, and that you care about them and their team."

Championship coaches are continually finding new material to motivate their players, whether it's reading material, quotes, stories, poems, videos, anything to get them fired up. Bringing in alumni or other coaches who have a story to tell is a great way to motivate. Jerry Kindall did this, as he describes: "I've had Bobby Knight address my team a couple times. Pete Rose came, before his suspension, he came to be the honorary manager of our all-pro alumni team. It's a fundraiser we have every spring. We invite back all the former Wildcats who are now in pro ball, big leagues, minors, whatever. And we invite an honorary manager to come manage that team. We've had Tommy Lasorda, Johnny Bench, Harmon Killebrew, and we had Pete Rose one year. We've done this for many years. It's a Sunday afternoon and the fans get into it. It's great inspiration to my players, and great reaffirmation of what we had been teaching."

Skip Bertman also brought guest speakers into the locker room to talk to players before a game. Generally it's a short talk, often from members of the community, who relate to the players how they became successful. Bertman was continually on the lookout for ways to motivate his guys. And obviously he found many ways!

Gaining Respect

It's been said that it's a greater compliment to be trusted than to be loved. That's because love is unconditional, while trust takes time, respect, care, and integrity. To gain the trust of the players, they need to believe the coach will do what he says and what he says is the right thing to do. When a player trusts that the coach has their best interests at heart, or at least the team's best interest, then the player is more likely to go full out. Sparky Anderson explains what worked for him in motivating players: "Honesty. Never lie to a player. I have coached 26 years in the major leagues, and I know that I never lied to a player. To me, that is the greatest gift you can give yourself as a coach. A gift that I will never lie to a player."

Mike Hargrove talks about gaining respect: "I think you get respect from players by being honest. If you're consistent in what you do, and you mix the right amount of sympathy with the right amount of hard-nosed iron will, then I think the players will accept what it is you do and respect what you do. I found that all athletes kind of have this 'button' behind their left ear, if you yell too much, they just flip it off. They still play hard, but they don't hear what you're saying. So consequently, I like the old theory of *Walk softly and carry a big stick*. It seems to help that when you do raise your voice, you bring home a point forcefully. It's done at the proper times and it gains their attention and I think players respect that, that you're not browbeating them all the time."

Gene Mauch talks about the exchange of respect: "I don't know any other way than just being fair. I've always felt like it was more important to the player himself to know that I respected him. The manager's job is to get the most out of the player. If the player knows that the manager respects him, the player will perform better than if the manager has his respect. The manager having that player's respect isn't going to help him on the field. But if a player knows he has the manager's respect, that's liable to promote him as a player."

Staying Positive

One of the common attributes of championship coaches is that they find ways to keep their players in a positive mindset. Motivating an individual with criticism or the threat of negative response may cause action, but to really take the person to the next level takes getting him to believe in himself and encouraging him when he gets down.

Davey Johnson explains how he gets it done: "The old dictatorial way of doing things doesn't cut it. It doesn't cut it in the minor leagues, and it doesn't cut it here.

There's a lot of teaching, but again, you have to have a lot of fun. You work hard to be able to perform to your potential, but you have to enjoy it—it's a game. This is not some WWII battle, I mean, it's a game. We're blessed to be the top athletes in the country to be able to play this game."

Over the course of a long season, there will be numerous times when players will be down on themselves or their teammates, and it's the coaches job to monitor that and maintain the desired atmosphere. Jim Lefebvre explains: "The key is this...when you play 192 ball games, don't ever let your team get down. You're hot, you're cold, you're hot, you're cold. When you're down, that's when you have to really pump them up, keep them loose and relaxed. A lot of managers have a tendency to get uptight. When you start to go into a losing cycle, the key is to get them loose and relaxed. Then, when you start winning, you can be a little stronger on them as far as doing things right. The key is when you start to get down a little bit, don't start hammering on your team about all the things they're doing wrong. Let's get back to thinking about what we have to do right. That's the key to keep motivating a ball club, handling those down moments. The good moments take care of themselves, and that means for players too. The team's playing well, but a player's down. Now, don't let that player die. Because he can start bringing other guys with him."

Bob Todd is careful with negative emotions. He explains: "There are a lot of times that the players don't have the type of game performance-wise that they want. I'll never say a word to them—better than chewing them out. I probably show very little emotion negatively. It's one of my pet peeves from a player's perspective and from a coach's perspective. There's no negative emotions shown on the field. The only emotion I want shown is a positive emotion... pat your teammates on the back, give him a hug, congratulate him by shaking his hand and, as a coach, it's the same thing I do. If a kid makes a mistake, he didn't make that mistake because he wanted to, so there's no negative emotion after the game or the next day. We might sit down and talk about why he made the mistake, but it's obvious to any athlete that they didn't want to go out there and make that mistake, so there's no reason to show any negative emotion to embarrass that person."

Jerry Kindall makes sure that his actions line up with his words. He emphasizes respecting players and demanding that players respect each other. This can be done verbally and nonverbally. He explains: "It's best to motivate the players by being encouraging and supportive. There are players that haven't handled authority very well. So we have to be constructively critical, certainly not abusive, not demeaning, but we have to, at times, get in their face in a constructively critical way. That's one part of coaching that's necessary. But for every time we do that, I maintain we need to give them five examples of support, encouragement, uplift and esteem. So I reminded myself constantly of that formula (5:1). If I'm on a player, and he is perhaps a little irritated with me that I'm continually trying to make him better, and I might lose my temper, regrettably, I want to give him five supports. They can be small things but they mean a lot to him. I may say, 'Good swing,' if I've been working with his swing or his infield play; I want to compliment, support, and encourage him. [For example,] things in the locker room: hand him a towel when he goes by on the way to the shower. Other small things you can do for that 5:1 formula: hold the door for them, we're not above holding the door for a player when we're walking in a room."

Appeal to Their Legacy

If you look at the people who have gained the most respect throughout history, it's those who have left a legacy. People like Gandhi, or Nelson Mandela, Martin Luther King Jr, or John F. Kennedy; they've changed the history of entire nations. Those people are remembered in textbooks because of their vision and leadership. In some way, big or small, everyone wants to be respected, acknowledged and remembered—it's the same with baseball players.

The twenty-fifth guy on the team may only play once a month, but if he works hard and inspires others, he'll be remembered with respect. It doesn't take any ability to work hard, to be conscientious, and to be a team player.

Ed Cheff strives to get his players to respect each other, if not like each other:

"I think a player's goal should always be a point of trying to earn someone else's respect. We talk about that all the time—in practice, off the field, social situations, whatever. One of the key points is that you always have their respect. Remind them that they'll never remember what you hit, they'll never remember your batting average, they're not going to remember those types of things about you; they're going to remember what type of person you were.

"I appeal to their legacy, what they're going to be known as—I use that a lot in motivation. 'What do you want to be remembered as? How are people going to remember you?' I think a lot of people are motivated by a legacy they want to leave. Some people don't start thinking about it until they're 40 or 50 years old.

"You have to look at 15 years from now, what kind of legacy would I leave here, what am I known as? I talk to kids about that—'What do you want to be known as when you leave here?' A player may say, 'I want to be known as a guy that everybody respected.' [I say,] 'Well, if you want to do that, then you can't do this and this, and you might think about this and this if you really want to be respected.' So we're trying to do that," Cheff explains.

Getting players to focus on their legacy forces players to look at the big picture. It takes them out of the me-me-me mode and gets them to think about how others will view them, how they'll be remembered, if they'll be respected in future years. When players work to gain the respect of their teammates, then they are setting themselves up for teamwork to be actualized.

Leaving a legacy for many players means putting their names up with the best that ever played there. Every rookie that has ever walked into Yankee Stadium has experienced the awe of those who have gone before him. The dream of being associated with those icons drives them. Dusty Baker explains: "Our locker room had Willie Mays, Willie McCovey, Juan Marichal, Bobby Bonds, Orlando Cepeda, Gaylord Perry and some of the bad boys that played there before. The picture is one thing, but the feeling that you remember is harder to take away than the pictures."

A Consequence For Every Action

To get there, to be associated with those icons that players have dreamed about takes an intense realization that every moment, every decision, and every action counts. And that every thought and action, however little, brings about a similar or responsive action or thought. These, in combination, create peoples lives. When the players get this, they can really move forward in their quest for greatness on the field, in the classroom, and in life.

Bob Todd explains: For every action that you do, there is a consequence. It may be positive or it may be negative. The majority of the time when there is a consequence that's going to be positive, most people get that feedback pretty quickly. If I swing the bat and get a hit, that's immediate. A lot of negative consequences to an action show up two weeks, three weeks, maybe even a month down the road, and those negative consequences come back to hurt you. They're not as immediate, so they're not fresh on your mind. Sometimes you can continue to make the same action cause the same negative consequence that hurts you down the road.

"I talk to our players about doing as much as they can so there's more positive consequences that are going to come back and help later, and that's tough. It's tough to relate that because [they think,] 'I'm abusing my body drinking beer and not eating right and this and that, but I'm hitting the ball good right now and I'm in the groove and I've been playing good baseball for 10 days. Heck with it; I'm not changing it.' But what's going to happen is three weeks down the road or a month down the road, it kind of catches up with you. I mean, lack of sleep and all of the sudden you're worn out and the bat's heavy and everything breaks loose. So, you need to keep everything in perspective which kind of goes back to the same thing you talk about in baseball. There's no ups and downs; try to keep an even keel. Baseball is such a challenging game, and that's the way life is. There's going to be lots of decisions you have to make, so for every action or every decision you make, there's going to be a positive or negative," Todd explains.

Find a Way Every Day

The decisions that players make are initially influenced by the atmosphere the coach has created, in the clubhouse, on the field, and off the field. If the coach is continually finding ways to stay positive, continually making good decisions and seeking excellence, then the players will see that.

Rod Delmonico tries to make good decisions every day that filter through the team: "Motivation starts with me as a coach. I've got to read whatever books I can, listen to whatever tapes are out there, any information I can get. I just try to find as much information as I can. Listen to any motivational speakers, any tapes they might have. You process it, take what's good for you and your program, and use it. Some things will not work, some will. You have to know the chemistry of your team.

"We have a mental log we keep in the locker room for our guys to read—a book with all kinds of poems, sayings, quotes, and phrases all about hitting, pitching, and life in general. Different quotes from anybody. A book that if you're down, there's something in there. If you're going good, there's something in there to keep you going. If you doubt yourself, there's something in there. It's just a mental book that I keep, and whenever I see something I like, a saying or a phrase, I put it in the book.

"To motivate, you have to say something daily to the kids and to the team in a positive way. Each day I try to pick kids up mentally. For example, this guy might not be giving me 100%, and I'll tell him, 'You could be the best hitter on the team if you just do these things.' What if? I think it's a mental thing every day to work on my guys to challenge them to get better. For me, that's motivating my team daily. You have to do it daily. I might hit the whole team with a mental thought, but individually, my coaches and I have to motivate them, keep them upbeat, and stay with them. And pick their game up, and get them better.

"We try to be as positive as we can, but it might mean motivating them in a negative way, challenging them a little bit. But you have to motivate daily. To me, you can go out and take ground balls and you can hit, but [you also need to] touch the mental part every day. It's like, 'We win in the seventh, eighth and ninth—they're going to make an error; they're going to kick the ball around, we're going to beat them in the seventh, eighth, and ninth.' It's important to share that with them. To some extent, whether it's individually or as a team, put a quote at the bottom [of the day's plan], or I might put a poem up in their locker about attitude. I put it in their locker so they can read it, and then it goes in the book."

Motivate For the Big Game

Preparation for the big game is no different than preparation for any game. If you've been to the World Series, do the same thing it took to get you there. Ed Cheff's pregame plan for mental preparation is doing just that: "Take a great infield, let's show these guys we can play, that's our strategy...have a great BP. I don't get into the 'rah-rah.' I couldn't give a 10-minute motivational speech before every game, I don't have anything to say. I'm not creative enough, it's just not me; I don't want to talk about it, let's just get prepared to play. Let's take a great infield, let's just bust our ass. I'm going to give you some divers, we're going to make some great plays, we're not going to yell and rah-rah, but we're going to work real hard on having a real good crisp infield."

Bob Todd discusses his pre-playoff game preparation: "Sometimes it depends on reading a team whether I need to kind of just say, 'Look, we have to work a little harder and stay focused to get 'em going,' but many times I have been sort of fortunate. The teams that I have had that have gone to the playoffs have usually been maybe too focused, too pumped up, and I have tried to take a little more of a relaxed approach right there. I try to get them to calm down and bring them back to a position where we have to keep our adrenaline and our actions under control. This is not a peaks and valleys game. I want you just as focused and just as happy and just as determined three days from now as we were at day one when we got into this tournament."

Principle #10
Motivate Daily

Motivation comes from implementing the *Ten Principles of Championship Teams*. When a team does the first nine, motivation naturally becomes an integral part of it all. Players become centered and focused because they work on seeking excellence and constant self-improvement. They have a covenant with themselves and their teammates that creates a very strong belief in who they are and their purpose, and they are motivated to work toward that purpose every day. This common purpose becomes an energy that propels them.

The energy burns like a fire, fueled by continually visualizing their future success. The fire needs to be controlled, never getting too high or too low. Great coaches teach champions how to control their minds and become mentally tough. They lock out the negatives and hone in on their goal with laser focus. They don't allow any deviation from that purpose, and with every setback they get back up and move on.

They do this because they have leaders on the team who push each other and police each other, maintaining a focused energy on the team. The head coach needs these leaders to motivate as much as he does, because the stories, the videos, the discipline, and the covenant are limited motivational tools. They need the leaders to fill in the gaps. It all must work together.

Players want to be motivated, they want to unite as a team, and they want to work hard. They know the feeling of being motivated, the greatness that comes with even a fleeting moment of motivation, and they remember the feeling and seek it. They know that true champions are a team in the true spirit of the word: they work together, they trust and respect each other, they impel each other to reach greater heights than they would alone; they have fun together, and they become better by the heightened senses they attain by following the Ten Principles.

Each of the Ten Principles relates to motivation, to getting the most out of each player, every pitch, every moment. The champions in this book have done that, and now have shared with you how to do it too, with their dugout wisdom.

APPENDIX

INDIVIDUALS WHO WERE INTERVIEWED FOR THIS BOOK

ADAMS, GARY – University of Southern California, Los Angeles (UCLA)

With over 1,000 victories in over 30 years of coaching (28 with UCLA), has collected four Pac-10 championships (1976, 1979, 1986, 2000), five second-place finishes, five third-place finishes, and three fourth-place finishes.

ANDERSON, SPARKY – Cincinnati Reds, Detroit Tigers

Managed for 26 years in the big leagues from 1970 – 1995, winning three World Series titles, two with the Big Red Machine ('75,'76) and one with the Detroit Tigers ('84). He won five league championships and was AL manager of the year in 1984 and 1987.

BAKER, DUSTY – San Francisco Giants, Chicago Cubs

Managed the Giants from 1993 through 2002, winning NL West titles in 1997 and 2000, and the NL pennant in 2002. Has won the NL manager of the year three times, in 1993, 1997, and 2000.

BENNETT, BOB - Fresno State University

Ranks as the seventh all-time winningest coach in NCAA Division I history. With a 1,302-759-4 record, Bennett closed out his career with 26 consecutive winning seasons, 17 conference championships, 21 NCAA Tournament berths, 32 All-Americans, nine first-round draft picks, two College World Series appearances, and three WAC Coach of the Year awards.

BERTMAN, SKIP - Louisiana State University

Retired in 2001 with an 870-330-3 record after 18 years with the Tigers. Took the Tigers to 11 College World Series. Won five national titles and was national Coach of the Year six times.

BLANEY, CHARLIE – Los Angeles Dodgers

Served in the Dodger's organization for over 30 years, most recently as the Dodger's president of minor league operations. Was instrumental in the Dodgers' nine National League Rookie of the year winners, including four in a row from 1979 to 1982, and five in a row from 1992 through 1996.

CHEFF, ED, - Lewis and Clark State University

Has a 1,307-358 win-loss record, entering the 2003 season. The Warriors' NAIA World Series championship in 2002 was the school's 12th since 1984. From 1982 to 1992, the Warriors played in 11 consecutive national championship games and won eight. More than 88 of Cheff's former players at Lewis and Clark have played professional baseball, and several have played in the big leagues, including four current major leaguers.

CLAIRE, FRED - Los Angeles Dodgers

Joined the Dodgers in 1969 and proved to be an award-winning executive at every stage of his 30-year career with the Dodgers. When the Dodgers won the World Series in 1988, Claire was named Major League Baseball's "Executive of the Year" by The Sporting News.

COLLINS, TERRY - Houston Astros, Anaheim Angels

Managed the Houston Astros from 1994 through 1996 and Anaheim '97 through '99.

COTTIER, CHUCK - Seattle Mariners

Played in the big leagues for nine seasons, before managing the Seattle Mariners in 1984, 1985, and 1986.

DEDEAUX, ROD - University of Southern California

He led the Trojans to an unprecedented 11 national titles, 28 conference championships, and an overall record of 1,332-571-11 his 45-year tenure at USC. Named Coach of the Year six times by the College Baseball Coaches Association, he was inducted into its Hall of Fame in 1970. Honored by Collegiate Baseball magazine as NCAA Division I Coach of the Century.

DELMONICO, ROD - University of Tennessee

Has eight 40-win seasons, including two 50-win campaigns. Has won an average of 41 games per year, two Southeastern Conference titles, two trips to the College World Series, six NCAA regional appearances four SEC Eastern Division crowns, and three SEC Eastern Division Tournament championships. Named Baseball America's 1995 National Coach of the Year and the SEC Coach of the Year in 1994 and 1995. The winningest coach in Tennessee baseball history.

DIERKER, LARRY - Houston Astros

Won the NL central division title four out of his five years in Houston ('97 through '01) and was 1998 NL manager of the year.

DIETZ, JIM – San Diego State University

Led SDSU to 25 winning seasons in 27 years and has taken his charges to eight NCAA Regional appearances. A member of the American Baseball Coaches Association (ABCA) Hall of Fame.

DOMBROWSKI, DAVE – Detroit Tigers, Florida Marlins

Currently, serves as the president/CEO/general manager of the Detroit Tigers. Led the Florida Marlins to a World Series Championship in 1997.

FRANCONA, TERRY – Philadelphia Phillies

Played ten years in the big leagues and managed the Philadelphia Phillies for four years from 1997 – 2000.

GARNER, PHIL – Milwaukee Brewers, Detroit Tigers

Played 16 seasons in the big leagues and was a member of the 1979 World Series Championship team – the Pittsburgh Pirates. He has managed in the big leagues for ten years with Milwaukee and Detroit.

GILLICK, PAT – Toronto Blue Jays, Baltimore Orioles, Seattle Mariners

Assembled the Toronto Blue Jays' World Series winning teams of 1992 and 1993 as their general manager. He also was general manager with the Baltimore Orioles in 1996 and 1997 when they reached the ALCS. He assumed the same position with the Seattle Mariners in 2001 they tied the all-time major-league record for wins with 116.

HARGROVE, MIKE – Cleveland Indians, Baltimore Orioles

Managed Cleveland from 1991 to 1999, and Baltimore from 2000 to present. Won two AL pennants in 1995 and 1997 with Cleveland.

HOUSE, TOM

Pitched from 1967 to 1979 for the Atlanta Braves, the Boston Red Sox, and the Seattle Mariners. He has coached since 1980 for the Houston Astros, San Diego Padres, Texas Rangers, and Chiba Lotte Marines (Tokyo). Perhaps, best known as Nolan Ryan's pitching coach, Tom travels the world as an international consultant, performance analyst, and sports psychologist. He is widely recognized as one of the game's foremost authorities on pitching.

HOWE, ART – Oakland A's, New York Mets

Managed Houston from 1989 through 1993, and Oakland from 1996 through 2002 winning the AL west title in 2000 and 2002. His athletics won and winning a league record 20 straight games in '02.

JOHNSON, DAVEY – New York Mets; Los Angeles Dodgers

Managed 14 years in the big leagues, winning the World Series in 1986 with the New York Mets. Won AL Manager of the Year Award in 1997 with the Baltimore Orioles.

KELLY, TOM – Minnesota Twins

Managed the Twins from 1986 until 2001, winning the World Series in 1987 and 1991. In 1991, he won the American League Manager of the Year Award.

KINDALL, JERRY – University of Arizona

Won three national crowns: 1976, 1980 and 1986. During his tenure from 1973 to '96, his Wildcat teams rang up 856 wins and 12 post-season appearances.

KNUTSON, KEN – University of Washington

Named the Pac-10 North Coach of the Year three times. Has led the Huskies to two Pacific-10 Conference championships, four Pac-10 Northern Division crowns, and two second-place finishes in ten years.

LAND, CARROLL

Has been honored numerous times for his contributions to the game, including serving as president of the American Baseball Coaches Association, and being named to the NAIA Hall of Fame, the ABCA Hall of Fame, and the United States Olympic Committee. Has also served as President of the NAIA in 1983. In 1993, he was named Citizen of the Year by the San Diego City Club. As head coach of the Crusader baseball team, his squad won back-to-back NAIA District 3 and Far West Region titles. Point Loma finished fifth at the 1994 NAIA College World Series, and third in 1993.

LEFEBVRE, JIM – Seattle Mariners

Played eight seasons for the Los Angeles Dodgers (1965 – 1972). Has managed in the big leagues for six years with Seattle, Chicago, and Milwaukee.

LEYLAND, JIM – Pittsburgh Pirates, Florida Marlins

Won the World Series with the Florida Marlins in 1997. Was named the NL Manager of the Year in 1990 and 1992.

LOPEZ, ANDY – Pepperdine University, University of Florida, University of Arizona

Coached Pepperdine to the 1992 College World Series title, the smallest NCAA Division I school ever to win it. Coached the Florida Gators to two SEC championships, five NCAA tournament berths, and two CWS appearances. Averaged 40 wins per season at Florida. Is one of eight coaches in NCAA Division I history to lead two different schools to the College World Series. His teams have appeared in the NCAA postseason tournament nine times. Three of his teams went on to Omaha and the College World Series.

MAUCH, GENE – California Angels

Played in the big leagues for nine years, before going on to a 27 year managerial career in the big leagues.

MURPHY, PAT – Arizona State University

Became the youngest collegiate coach to reach 500 career victories in 1998. Currently, with over 600 wins, Murphy is the winningest active baseball coach under the age of 43 at any collegiate level. He also led the Holland Olympic team as they defeated Cuba at the 2000 Sydney Olympics, handing Cuba it's first-ever loss in Olympic history.

POLK, RON – Mississippi State University

Has a 1,122-534 (.678) overall record In 28 years as a collegiate head coach, and 360-238 (.602) mark in SEC games. His teams have made 18 NCAA tournament appearances and have earned seven College World Series berths. He has coached 28 All-Americans and 65 All-SEC players. Over 122 of his former players have signed professional baseball contracts, 15 of whom have advanced to the major leagues. Twice honored as the National Coach of the Year (1973 and 1985). One of only two head coaches in the history of college baseball to guide three different teams to the College World Series.

SABEAN, BRIAN – San Francisco Giants

Currently serves as the senior vice president and general manager of the San Francisco Giants. Led the Giants from last place in 1996 to first place in 1997, and six outs from winning the World Series in 2002.

STITT, JERRY – University of Arizona

Inducted into the Pima County (AZ) Sports Hall of Fame, Stitt spent 27 years as a player, assistant coach, and head coach at the University of Arizona. Stitt's teams batted a combined .327 under his guidance. Furthermore, 53 of his position players were drafted into professional baseball during his tenure as a coach at UA. As an assistant coach under former Wildcat skipper Jerry Kindall, Stitt helped Arizona to two national titles, four College World Series appearances, and three Pac-10 titles.

TIDROW, DICK – San Francisco Giants

Currently, serves as the Giants' vice president of player personnel. Pitched in the major leagues for 13 years, including three World Series' in a row, 1975-1977, with the New York Yankees.

TODD, BOB – The Ohio State University

Named the Big Ten Coach of the Year four times. Every player he has recruited to play at Ohio State has left the University with a championship ring. The winningest coach in 119 years of OSU baseball. OSU has won the conference championship six times and the conference tournament on five occasions. Todd has guided the Buckeyes to a berth in the NCAA Tournament in nine of his 15 seasons.

TOWERS, KEVIN – San Diego Padres

Currently, serves as the Padres executive vice president (2000-present) and general manager (1995-present). Helped lead the Padres to NL West titles in 1996 and 1998 and the NL pennant in 1998.

TREBELHORN, TOM – Milwaukee Brewers, Chicago Cubs, Baltimore Orioles

Managed in the big leagues for seven years from 1986 through 1991 with the Milwaukee Brewers and 1994 with the Chicago Cubs. Currently the third base coach for the Baltimore Orioles.

WETZEL, TERRY – Kansas City Royals

Was the scouting director for the Royals from 1997 – 2000.

ENDNOTES

Chapter 1

1. Johann Wolfgang von Goethe (1749-1832) German poet, dramatist, novelist, and scientist.

Chapter 2

1. Riley, Pat, *The Winner Within*, 1993, Riles and Company, Inc., p. 57.

Chapter 3

1. Allman, William, F. "The Mental Edge," August 3, 1992, *U.S. News and World Report*.

2. Badger, T.A., "Kobe's Done It In His Dreams," May 13, 2002, Associated Press.

3. Bertman led LSU to five College World Series championships: 1991, 1993, 1996, 1997, 2000.

4. During Bertman's last season at LSU (2001), he let the author in the locker room for the pre-game pep talk and video before a regional playoff game.

5. Allman, William, F. "The Mental Edge," August 3, 1992, *U.S. News and World Report*.

6. Swofford, Scott, producer, Merrill, Kieth, producer/director, *Olympic Glory*, 1999, Imax Films.

7. Musashi, Miyamoto, *The Book of Five Rings*, 1993, Shambhala Publications, Inc.

8. Slusser, Susan, "Big Comebacks Nothing New to Angels," October 27, 2002, *San Francisco Chronicle*

Chapter 4

1. In 1987, Andre Dawson became the only player in major league history to win an MVP for a last-place club. In 2002, Alex Rodriguez batted .300 with 57 home runs and 142 RBIs (leading the AL in the latter two categories) and failed to win the MVP.

2. Lesko, Wayne A., *Readings in Social Psychology*, 1994, Allyn and Bacon, p. 155, 156.

3. Outward Bound is an organization with programs that emphasize personal growth and teamwork through experiences and challenges, generally in a wilderness setting.

Chapter 5

1. Will, George, F., *Men at Work*, 1990, Harper Perennial, p. 187.

Chapter 6

1. Bennis, Warren, *On Becoming a Leader*, 1995, Addison Wesley, audiotape.

2. Loehr, James, E., *Mental Toughness Training for Sports*, 1982, Stephen Greene Press, p.12.

3. Loehr, James, E., *Mental Toughness Training for Sports*, 1982, Stephen Greene Press, p.75.

4. Canfield, Jack; Hanson, Mark Victor; and Hewitt, Les, *The Power of Focus*, 2000, Health Communications, Inc.

5. Will, George, F., *Men at Work*, 1990, Harper Perennial.

Chapter 7

1. Dorrance, Anson, *Training Soccer Champions*, 1996, JTC Sports, Inc.

Chapter 8

1. Loehr, James, E., *Mental Toughness Training for Sports*, 1982, Stephen Greene Press.

2. Musashi, Miyamoto, *The Book of Five Rings*, 1993, Shambhala Publications, Inc.

3. Loehr, James, E., *Mental Toughness Training for Sports*, 1982, Stephen Greene Press, p.78.

4. To a point. The goal is to go from the fastest beta waves, where the mind is overengaged and has tension, to slower beta waves and even alpha waves, where the mind is more relaxed but alert and clear thinking.

5. Proper deep breathing is diaphragmatic. During inhalation the ribs expand, as opposed to chest breathing, which is shallow and weak.

6. Covey, Stephen, R., *The Seven Habits of Highly Successful People*, 1989, Simon and Schuster, p. 133.

7. Useem, Jerry, "How to Manage Like Joe," April 30, 2001, *Fortune Magazine*.

Chapter 9

1. Armstrong, Lance, *It's Not About the Bike*, 2000, Putnam.

2. Useem, Jerry, "How to Manage Like Joe," April 30, 2001, *Fortune Magazine*.

ABOUT THE AUTHOR

Jim Murphy, MHK, CSCS*D, CPT*D, is an author, speaker, coach, and owner/operator of Murphy Fitness, a Vancouver, British Columbia, based company (www.murphyfitness.com). An NSCA certified strength and conditioning specialist, he has been involved in pro baseball for seven years, playing in the Chicago Cubs organization, before moving on to scouting and coaching. He received his undergraduate degree in psychology from the University of Washington and his graduate degree in human kinetics at the University of British Columbia. At UBC, he started the Thunderbirds' baseball team for the University, which is now a member of the NAIA. He also became the NSCA baseball division chairman and is the past NSCA director for British Columbia. At the 2000 Sydney Olympics, as the hitting and conditioning coach, Jim helped lead South Africa to a stunning upset victory over the Netherlands, knocking them out of any chance for a medal.

Jim also works for Major League Baseball International, putting on clinics around the world to promote the game of baseball. Jim has previously written for publications such as *The New York Daily News*, *World Series Magazine*, *Collegiate Baseball Magazine*, www.mlb.com, and the *Journal of Strength and Conditioning Research*.